SURVIVAL AND BEYOND:
A MAN'S GUIDE TO DIVORCE

Survival and Beyond: A Man's Guide to Divorce

Ethan S. Sharvit

iUniverse, Inc.

New York Bloomington Shanghai

Survival and Beyond: A Man's Guide to Divorce

iUniverse books may be ordered through booksellers or by contacting:

iUniverse
1663 Liberty Drive
Bloomington, IN 47403
www.iuniverse.com
1-800-Authors (1-800-288-4677)

Because of the dynamic nature of the Internet, any Web addresses or links contained in this book may have changed since publication and may no longer be valid.

The views expressed in this work are solely those of the author and do not necessarily reflect the views of the publisher, and the publisher hereby disclaims any responsibility for them.

ISBN: 978-0-595-51098-6 (pbk)
ISBN: 978-0-595-61764-7 (ebk)

Printed in the United States of America

CONTENTS

Acknowledgments

This book would not have been possible without the input of the men who agreed to share their divorce experiences with me. Sometimes they may have felt that I was giving of myself and helping them, when in fact, they were the ones who were doing the giving. They helped me understand that I was not alone, and gave me the inspiration to share that fact with others who have lost hope.

Special thanks to two people who were by my side the whole way: my one and only lawyer, Deborah, and my ex-boss and life-friend Bruce. I could not imagine anyone fighting harder for me than Deborah; she was able to get me through some really tough times with her commitment, loyalty and sensibility. If I was in a foxhole with one other person, I would be lucky if it were Deborah. Bruce was understanding during the entire process and was more flexible a boss than I could have wished for. I'll always remember his kindness and support during this painful time in my life.

And finally, I do not have enough words to express my appreciation and love to my family who stood by me during the divorce. I don't know if I would be here today without their help.

CHAPTER 1

▼

DIVORCE

On a warm, sunny morning in the heart of a sticky New York City summer, I found myself sitting on a hard, wood bench in an overcrowded courtroom. I checked my watch nervously every two minutes and prayed that my lawyer would walk in and join me soon. On the other side of the room sat my wife, along with other members of her family. Her lawyers were already there. I continued to watch the clock as rivulets of sweat trickled down my forehead. My shirt was drenched and I was glad for the sports jacket that I wore since it hid the sweat marks. I tried to maintain a cool facade. Back then, I had no notion about how these things worked and no idea that the court sessions always started later than scheduled.

I listened closely as the judge reprimanded a defense lawyer who had managed to annoy him. "Don't tell me about newspapers," he shouted. "I am not interested in becoming famous. Tell me about the law. The law."

An important meeting was being held at work without me, and I hoped that my absence would not be too obvious to my co-workers. I knew that it was important to be at the meeting, but this court appearance simply could not be changed. I had explained the situation to my boss and he understood what was going on; nevertheless, he wished that I could have been there with him because he would have liked my input.

Seated before me on his throne was the man who would decide how the next few years of my life would be played out. He did not know me, nor did he care to know me. He only wanted to know "the law."

That day, as I sat in the courtroom, I realized that nothing had prepared me for this moment. Sure, I had spoken with my lawyer on a few occasions. I had listened to war story after war story that many of my divorced buddies had shared with me. Some told me how they "got her good" or were "beaten" by her crooked and slimy lawyer.

And here I was, waiting for *my* case to be heard, and despite my seemingly calm demeanor, I was scared to death.

The setting was intimidating, and I was overwhelmed at the significance of the decisions that would soon be made. Mostly, I felt that I was all alone and that little by little I was falling apart.

These feelings are nearly universal, shared by many men who have gone through a divorce or who are in the midst of one. Advice, always well meant yet sometimes ill advised, pours in from all corners of the earth. Yet, nothing can truly prepare you for the changes that accompany a divorce.

As I felt lost and confused, so too will multitudes of men after me as they enter into this new and often dismal chapter of their lives and try to figure out what exactly is going on.

I wished that I had somehow prepared myself better. I wished that I had known what to expect. Mostly, I wondered why no one had told me about how I might feel when my life would be snatched out of my hands and my future determined by strangers in dark suits in a harsh and dusty courtroom.

Let's look at divorce by way of analogy. Picture a high-rise building standing proudly and prominently for a number of years. Every day, hundreds if not thousands of people spend the workday inside, some making their fortunes, others losing theirs and still others just struggling to maintain the status quo. Because of the many hours they spend there, many consider the building to be a home away from home. It was familiar, even comforting.

Now, imagine that same building being destroyed. Perhaps there was structural damage to the building and the authorities deemed it to be unsafe. Crowds gather to watch the edifice exploding in a grand commotion of sparks and fire.

The architect of the building, the person whose design laid the foundation for it and who spent months or even years overseeing its creation, watches in despair. It does not matter to him whether or not there was a legitimate reason for the destruction, such as irreparable structural damage that threatened life and limb. It would not matter to him that the demolition would save many innocent lives in the future. Here stands a person who invested a part of himself into the building, and now as he watches, it falls apart. His soul is wounded and he is prostrated by the devastation.

The dissolution of a marriage is no different. So much time and effort has been invested; yet now the investors see their hopes and dreams destroyed. It does not matter whether there is a good reason for the divorce or not. It does not matter who initiated the separation or why the separation took place. The end of a marriage is a distressing event and casts a shadow on the lives of those involved. Emotions run high on both sides; at times, the parties involved feel as if they have become different people, horrible versions of themselves that they would not have recognized only a few months before. Friendships are polarized and those that were once called your "relatives" will not speak to you again.

In essence, divorce represents death. The union of two people had given birth to a new life, and the divorce process sentences that life to death. This concept transcends fault and blame. When someone you love has died, it does not matter if more could have been done to save that person. The "what if" flies out the window when you are confronted with a dead body. So too with divorce. No matter how bad the marriage might have been, the divorce is the cessation of life as you know it. No matter what your particular circumstances may be, the divorce will be a difficult and trying experience.

Let's take my friend Robert. Robert was married to his high school sweetheart. At first, he felt that things were going just fine, but slowly, his relationship with his wife soured. Robert and his wife had changed as people and decided that they simply could not make each other happy. They decided to divorce amicably.

Sounds like a simple case. They should both be happier, right? Nevertheless, I witnessed the opposite effect. Robert had not prepared himself for the change that was about to occur in his life. He did not understand all the issues that would have to be resolved, nor did he remember what it was like to live alone. Most importantly, he missed the point that before he could move on with his life, he would have to confront the fact that his divorce was not a simple matter. His feelings of sadness contradicted the joy he had anticipated at escaping an unhappy marriage. He was confused and did not know where to turn.

This does not imply that one should not get divorced. I am not here to judge you, blame you or act as a marriage counselor. On the contrary; I am simply stating a fact about what divorce represents, and I am hopeful that recognizing this fact will help reconcile your feelings with the realities that you will soon face, as it helped me understand my own.

Unlike death, there is no funeral to bury the marriage. Friends and relatives will not console you. There will be no mourning period.

Instead, chances are that you will be thrust into new and unfamiliar situations. Life altering changes will be taking place at lightning speeds, and feelings of help-lessness will consume you. You will be forced to muster all of your strength in order to survive.

I too was consumed by the process of divorce. The issues that I faced seemed rather simple and clear-cut to me. However, before long, I found myself asking the following questions:

- When will it ever end?

- What has become of my life?

- Why am I so down all the time?

- What does the future hold for me?

My divorce truly transformed my life. One day I was a married, successful man with a child and a bright future. I lived in a nice apartment and was proud that I was supporting myself and my family. The next moment I found myself living in a room in my parents' house, unable to pay my legal fees, missing my daughter, depressed and alone. I was afraid of what the future would bring, and worst of all, I was full of uncertainty and fear.

Over the span of the next few years, I learned the complexities of divorce the hard way. I also learned that I was a survivor. I somehow found the strength deep within me to keep my head up and stay alive so that someday I would be able to enjoy life again. I found that by being pushed to extreme limits, I was able to become stronger and better able to face whatever lay ahead.

You too have the power to survive this process and live to tell about it. You are not the first man to go through a divorce; more importantly, you are not alone.

Through the practical steps presented in this book, I hope to prepare you for what you will face. Through the inspiration that I hope to impart, I intend to awaken your own strength that lies deep within you.

I will describe divorce experiences so that when you face similar ones yourself, you will not panic or lose your cool. Most of all, I hope to make the divorce pro-cess a little bit easier for you and help you believe that someday there will be light at the end of the tunnel.

In this book, I have set out to create a starting point for men who are embarking upon the painful journey of divorce. By reading about the experiences of others, you will be better equipped to face similar circumstances. Fear of the unknown can be crippling; here, I have set out to transform the unknown into the familiar. When you face these situations yourself, you will have the ability to draw on these experiences and gain strength from the knowledge that you are not alone and that you are now prepared and ready for whatever presents itself next.

As I outline what can be gained by reading the practical advice outlined in this book, let me begin by laying some ground rules as to what this book is "not" intended to do, and by doing so, explain exactly what you can gain by reading it.

I am *not* a matrimonial attorney and this book is not meant as a legal thesis on matters relating to divorce. On that topic, you can find a tremendous amount of information available through a variety of different sources. While I expound upon the importance of educating yourself on these matters, my purpose is not to lay down the law within the pages of this book. Laws relating to divorce will differ from state to state. Every divorce case is unique and will raise some distinct legal questions that require analysis and interpretation. After reading the section titled, "Choose Wisely—Getting a Lawyer That's Right For You," I am hopeful that your lawyer will have the competence to advise you as to your rights and the expected resolutions to pertinent issues should they be decided in a court of law or through joint settlement by both parties.

Despite the uniqueness of every divorce case, there are some general features that are common to most, if not all cases.

In the chapter on 'Facing Reality,' I outline some facts that you should be aware of. By facing reality as early as possible, you stand a better chance of surviving the ordeal with all of your pieces in tact and coming out with the best resolution possible. You will also be able to remain calm when events occur that you would otherwise not have been prepared for.

There are some universal steps that can be taken today that will help you along, no matter what specific issues you will face in the future. In addition, there are some issues that a majority of you will face in the coming weeks, months or even years that will require some type of resolution, including decisions on who will keep the house and how much alimony will be paid.

These two areas are highlighted in the sections titled "What You Can Do— Right Now!" and "Topics of Divorce."

In the former, I outline some practical steps that you can take today that will help you through the divorce. These steps do not entail legal strategies and plans of attack as to how to win your case. They are steps that will help bring some organization back to your life, at a time when you may feel that chaos reigns. These methods cannot be found in a divorce attorney's manual or in any motions to the court. Yet, following them are essential to you and can mean the difference between a hellish experience and a mere unpleasant one.

Next, in "Topics of Divorce," I set out to give you a taste of the various issues you will face. By acquiring a basic understanding, I hope to spare you the confusion and surprise that you might experience when the other side brings up an issue. I will not expound upon the legal writings on each issue, nor tell you what you should strive for as a minimum or maximum resolution for each. Instead, I hope to familiarize you with the topics that typically arise during a divorce.

These discussions should get you thinking about the areas that you must specifically focus on in your own divorce. As the issues become clearer, I will discuss the importance of knowing what you want to get out of the divorce in the section titled "Focus on True Interests." There, I outline the difference between a true interest that you have and a firm stance that you might adopt, a distinction that will help you formulate and express your true desires.

I am *not* a licensed psychologist or marriage counselor. I am not here to judge you or give any advice as to how to make a marriage work. You will not read here of the holy sanctuary called marriage, nor that there is still hope. If you are taking steps to salvage your marriage, I commend you. You can certainly talk to your Rabbi or Priest and see if there is something that can be done to save the marriage. You can find a tremendous amount of material on the subject of reconciliation that others have written with the best of intentions, but which might do you no good in your present state. This book is intended for those men who are facing divorce today and are in need of guidance.

When the decision has already been made that divorce is the only option available to you, the practical steps and words of encouragement contained in this book will be there to help you through a bleak time in your life.

Now, if I am neither a lawyer nor a marriage counselor, who am I and how can I help you?

To state it as simply as I can, I hope to be your friend. I am a man that has gone through a life-changing event. I took the experience to heart and believe that there is much that you can gain by hearing about it. I have set out to better prepare you for what you will likely face, and most importantly, inspire you in a way that will help you to survive this trying time in your life to live and breathe another day.

I have gone through it and I know how difficult it can be. For this reason, my goal is to lessen your burden and ease your suffering as much as possible. Familiarizing yourself with the process is invaluable. I have also learned that as surely as morning follows night, a better life awaits you after your divorce. Knowing this will give you something to look forward to and anticipate.

Imagine that I am sitting next to you in your favorite bar or café. We are having a beer or one of your favorite drinks. A baseball game is blaring in the background. We can kick back and relax as only two men can.

Fill in the blanks, but make yourself comfortable. I am with you now as a friend, not an adversary, trying to share with you the insights that have helped me and others get through a tumultuous time in their lives. We are united in our suffering, and we will be united in our survival.

I have been asked, "Why only men?"

I answer very simply, *"I am a man."* As a man, I recognize that my own experiences are shaped by my perceptions, and as such, I feel comfortable sharing them with other men. Sure, women should feel free to read this book, but I have shied away from making my own experiences more universal and applicable to women by altering them in any way.

I know that I am biased toward men, and I am comfortable with that viewpoint and not about to change it. If that means that my potential reader base is limited at the onset, so be it.

From the nature of this book it might be difficult for me to make the claim that I fully understand women. To me, women represent a different species, one that is worth learning about since their presence might enhance a man's life in a variety of ways. This is not the time or the place for such an education.

It is also a well-accepted fact that in general, men have a harder time than women in expressing their thoughts and feelings. Women are active in developing their own support systems and listening to one another's troubles and hardships. Men are different. They tend to keep their feelings to themselves and bottle up their hurt. Oftentimes, there is no outlet for a man to express his feelings except through getting angry and losing control.

I have written this book with these men in mind. While it may be difficult for the male brutes that we are to express our thoughts, I am hopeful that you men will have the opportunity to gain strength through the trials and tribulations of those who have suffered before you.

It may be difficult to ask a male friend for advice on divorce. The topic in and of itself is personal and often embarrassing; I hope to answer some of the questions that you have and save you from the shame of exposing your fears to the world. There are thousands out there who, just like you, are searching for answers and help. I plan to give it to you here and now. Relax, open up your mind to new ideas and experiences, and be brave as you begin the journey.

CHAPTER 2

▼

FACING REALITY

In this chapter, I focus on facing the realities of your predicament. You accept the fact that you are going to get divorced. That decision might have been yours alone, or you and your spouse may have made it collectively. Perhaps the decision was thrust upon you at a time when you least expected it. At this point, it really does not matter.

The fact is that there is now a job that must be done, and you should begin to prepare yourself for the task at hand. Your actions over the next few weeks and months will dictate the way you live your life for years to come, and the decisions that you make right now may be the most important decisions that you have ever had to make in your entire life.

In the next few sections, I will ask you to:

- "Shift Gears" away from your emotions and towards business

- "Get to OK" when settling on a final agreement

- Recognize what "The Court System" means to you

Understanding the specifics of these three topics will set you on your way toward establishing realistic expectations for the process that you will soon learn so much about.

Before I begin, there are a few basic facts that warrant your attention.

First and foremost, the process of divorce takes time. There is no other way to say it and I can't sugarcoat it for you. Some of your friends might tell you that you can do it in a month or two. Don't listen to them, and don't establish such unrealistic goals at the onset. Forget what you have heard and prepare yourself for the real thing.

The fact is that most divorces take years to finalize, not months. Think about the length of separation, either physical or emotional, and the time spent going to marriage counselors in hopes of saving the marriage. This period alone could last years.

Some divorces will take a number of months, while many others will take a number of years. I am not stating this to frighten or overwhelm you. However, I would rather you face facts here and now than be shocked later on. You should prepare for the worst so that you do not succumb to any surprises. If the divorce is finalized relatively quickly, then you can breathe a sigh of relief and congratulate yourself. If not, you will have already prepared yourself accordingly and will take this in stride. With so many important issues hanging in the balance, it is not always wise or recommended to rush the process either. You are generally looking for a reasonable resolution, not merely a speedy one.

To decrease your anxiety level, I recommend that you **not** put a mental time limit or an 'expected resolution date' on your divorce. Such a deadline can only lead to increased stress as you approach your pre-determined doomsday. Instead, work diligently toward closure while understanding that the process will reach its end when the time is right. Of course there will be a final resolution, but adding time limits to yourself in your current state will only hurt you in the future. There is so much that you must do now, including staying focused on various motions to the court. Each of these will have their own strict deadlines. You certainly do not need the added pressure of self-imposed timelines hanging over your head.

Many in your circle will not understand this. Well-meaning friends and family members will ask you, "So? Is it over yet? I never heard of someone's divorce taking such a long time! What's the problem?" They mean well, but ignore them just the same. You do not have to explain yourself to everyone that you meet or justify the amount of time that the divorce is taking. That is your business.

I suggest a reply in the following tone, "We're working on it."

Leave it at that, and don't bother to tell them that the divorce will be completed in January or February or any other month. Stay clear of final deadlines, and focus on the short-term steps that require your immediate attention.

Second, the process of divorce is a painful one. Many of you are strong, confident, and successful men. Others may be less so. ***It does not matter how tough you are.*** Divorce hurts everyone.

I will share the experience of a man who was recently divorced:

"The past two years were the worst years of my life. I dreaded waking up in the morning. I dreaded stepping outside. I was depressed all the time. I hated life, and I hated my wife, and I hated myself."

These words might seem a bit extreme, but they accurately reflect the sentiments of many men who are going through divorce. The joy of life is lost (albeit temporarily), and happiness is hard to come by.

I too felt depressed and confused during the divorce process. I did not want to see anyone or do anything. In short, I hurt in a way that I had never experienced before. But that was the whole point. It was my first experience with true pain, and I did not know how to handle it.

I hope that your experience will be a more positive one. I will help you understand some of the things that are going on around you and deal with them in an effective way. I will try to give you the power to make the most out of the situation and survive the ordeal with all of your vital organs in tact. But remember, anticipating the worst-case scenario will serve you well and save you from painful realizations down the road. As such, I want there to be no misconceptions. There will be no magic tricks to help you. You will need to work hard and devote your time and energy toward the process. It will hurt like never before, but you will come out a stronger and wiser man. I will return to this matter in the last section of the book and hopefully inspire you to make it through this period of your life and overcome any obstacles.

To summarize, a divorce can take a tremendous amount of time and effort, and the process can be an extremely painful one. Do not set unrealistic expectations. Understand the possible ways that your divorce might go, including a worst-case scenario and a best-case scenario, and then concentrate your efforts on preventing the worst from actually happening.

Shifting Gears

During the course of any divorce, emotions run high on both sides of the fence. This is only natural. Family members and friends get involved and add their two cents whenever they can. Feelings of love and companionship are replaced by spitefulness and hate, while at the same time, life-altering changes and decisions are at stake.

You must now begin to draw a clear distinction between emotions and the reality of the divorce proceedings. Understand that the divorce will culminate in a final, legal document. It is in essence a contract, like any other contract that is negotiated in the world of business, and you must shift gears accordingly in the face of this simple fact.

Visualize yourself in a racecar. You have reached exceedingly high speeds and shifted to the highest gear. The speedometer is advancing before your eyes, and the scenery outside is blurred. Unexpectedly, a roadblock appears up ahead. You act quickly. You step on the break pedals and shift the gears downward to decrease your speed and avoid a head-on collision.

So too today, you have no choice but to shift gears and adjust to the circumstances that have presented themselves. You must begin by adjusting your way of thinking about the divorce. Up to now you have made some heart wrenching decisions or perhaps some of these decisions have been made for you. You have been on an emotional roller coaster, one that you never hoped to ride.

I do not have the power to tell you to stop having these feelings. You undoubtedly will feel many emotions during the divorce process. What *you must do*, however, is start viewing the divorce from a different perspective.

Ask yourself these questions:

- What would you do if you were involved in a multi-million dollar transaction?

- Would you stand silently by while decisions were made and the contract written up?

- Is your divorce as important as a task at work?

I venture to say that your divorce is as important to you as any other work project you have ever been faced with. If confronted with a significant transaction, you would actively research the issues, read every word of the contract carefully and make sure that your interests are met in the final document. You would work with your business associates in a manner that befits a professional and not act out on every emotion that you feel.

In order to do this during the divorce proceedings, you must learn to separate yourself from the transaction. This is easier said than done, but if you focus your energy properly, you will find that it is within your power to develop this skill.

Your lawyers, along with the lawyers representing your wife, are now your business associates. The person that you viewed as your life partner is now your business partner. All of these parties must be dealt with in a professional and respectful manner, despite what you may feel about them.

Another way to think about this, in your own "man's terms" is that the divorce is a "project," such as building a deck or adding a new room to your house. In each case, you would prepare for the project, allot time for working on the project, ask advice from those who have performed a similar task in the past and execute your plan. Why should your divorce be any different or less important in any way than one of your home or work projects? Aren't you more important than a deck or report for your boss? Don't you deserve to treat your life with at least the same degree of seriousness that you give your job?

Take the case of Brian, a friend of mine, who is a professional investment banker. After three years of marriage, Brian had separated from his wife and was beginning the process of getting a divorce. At the well-known investment bank where he worked, Brian was involved with billion dollar deals in his mergers & acquisitions group and was a rising star in his division. He knew how to close a deal and get a contract finalized.

When going through his divorce, he would show up at his lawyer's office with an entirely different demeanor. He would take off his tie and jacket, slump down in the chair and look dumbfounded. He would be short-tempered and appear agitated, checking his watch every few minutes and staring out the window.

After a few such sessions, Brian's lawyer made a simple yet poignant remark, "I thought you were a big-time deal closer. Still, I would hate to be one of your clients. Just look at you. You look and sound like a bum."

Brian was taken aback. He asked himself, "Would he treat a merger the same way that he was treating his divorce?" "Would he run away from a challenge?" Not a chance.

From that day forward, Brian treated his divorce with the same degree of professionalism that he treated his other 'deals' in the workplace and was ultimately able to reach an agreement that he was satisfied with.

Now take the case of Josh. For months, Josh stated over and over again that he would not, under any circumstances, pay any alimony. "No matter what," he said, "I will never pay alimony." After numerous sessions, Josh's lawyer finally told him that either he faced reality or found someone else to represent him. Josh had been supporting his wife for fifteen years. She did not work nor did she have any work related skills. She took care of the house and the children during the marriage and enjoyed a high standard of living. In all likelihood, Josh would be forced to pay alimony. His lawyer told him that he couldn't change the law. If he refused to be realistic and reach a compromise, a judge would eventually make the decision anyhow and force Josh to pay.

Blinded by emotions, Josh was unwilling to face facts and recognize that the law was not on his side. If he were able to face reality earlier, Josh would have been able to save himself thousands of additional dollars in legal fees and weeks of unnecessary haggling.

The point that I am making is not that you should just give up and throw in the white towel. You have every right to go after what you want with all of your strength and ability. You must, however, have a basis on which to stand. If you allow your emotions to dictate your decisions, you will ultimately suffer for it. I implore you to face reality sooner rather than later and keep your emotions in check and out of the courtroom as much as possible.

I, like my friend Brian, needed a jolt to my system to reign in my emotions and focus on the contract that I was helping to write. Until I shifted gears from the emotional elements of the divorce to the business and contractual elements, I was unable to see clearly. A part of me wanted to be vengeful and spiteful, and I was blind to the practical realities that were staring me in the face. Luckily for Brian and I, our lawyers helped stress the need to shift gears and view the divorce in a practical and businesslike way.

Why wait for someone down the road to bring you back on track? Why allow yourself to be driven by emotions and blind to the realities of your situation? The longer it takes you to get a grip on the situation, the more money and time you will waste.

Start today by taking control of the divorce process and changing your own mindset. Divorce your feelings from the project that you have undertaken.

You should not only view the divorce as a business contract, you must recognize that it is one of the most vital contracts that you will ever enter into. More importantly, there is zero tolerance for failure. You cannot choose to walk away from it or let your lawyer handle everything. By acting with the same level of professionalism that you would give your business partners and colleagues, you will increase your chances of success dramatically and hopefully reach a resolution that you can live with.

Getting to "OK"

You have begun to think about the divorce in terms of a business transaction and are focusing your attention on detaching yourself emotionally from the project at hand. It is now time to dig a little deeper into the type of transaction that you are in the process of negotiating and establish the proper perspective on the divorce.

What type of contract is the divorce really comparable to? How should you view the proceedings? What should you hope for?

Imagine that a relative or close friend has recently passed away. You are sitting in the office of the funeral director discussing the details of the funeral that will take place tomorrow morning.

Despite the solemnity and gravity of the matter at hand, details have to be worked out. You will make decisions as to what type of casket to purchase, where to bury the body, and the type of program that will be followed during the service. In addition, monetary issues will emerge, negotiations will take place, and payments will be made. These are not issues that you want to deal with in your moment of sorrow; nevertheless, they must be resolved and finalized quickly and efficiently.

Now, let's think about your feelings in relation to such a negotiation. When you place your signature on the dotted line and agree with the funeral director on all of the details, will you be joyous? Can the agreement itself be celebrated in the same way that you would celebrate the signing of a purchase contract, such as the purchase of a new home or a brand new car?

The situation is much different and calls for a unique response. A person in such a negotiation would likely hope for fairness and reasonableness. He certainly does not want to get taken advantage of. He will not, however, haggle over small details or celebrate what he perceives to be "a great deal." The seriousness of the situation would preclude one from viewing the negotiation in such a manner and help him set more grounded and realistic expectations.

Some men go into their divorce proceedings with the notion that it is a contest and that they can somehow "win." Some are determined to win at all costs, but are not concerned with the damage they will inflict along the way. They view the divorce as a competitive game and strive to emerge victorious. Such viewpoints are harmful and inappropriate. Would such expectations and viewpoints make sense in relation to the case of a relative in mourning arranging the details of the funeral? Does the word "win" even apply? Would anyone in his right mind set out to trick or deal unjustly with the funeral director?

Just as these types of feelings are not applicable to the above situation, they are not applicable to divorce. In a divorce, no one really wins. You should strive for an agreement that is just and in keeping with legal constraints—no excitement, no victory.

With this in mind, I have termed the phrase, "Getting to OK." In a national bestseller on the art of principled negotiation titled, Getting to Yes, the authors outline a method of negotiation where two parties can reach agreement in a principled and creative fashion. By developing options, Win-Win situations emerge and both sides are pleased with the results of the negotiations. They work together towards "Getting to Yes."

As a fan of the book and an avid follower, I can tell you that I have personally benefited from this method. However, in relation to divorce, it is important to set realistic expectations up front to avoid disappointment in the future. I believe that your expectations would be better thought of as "Getting to OK," a slimmed down version of the original. By getting to "OK," you will be cognizant of the realistic goals that should be set and remain true to them.

When a buyer and a seller of a home discuss the details of the purchase contract, there is usually some give and take on both sides. Compromises are made, and the deal is struck. Ultimately, the goal is to reach a settlement that both sides can live with and feel comfortable with. The buyer should feel that he paid a fair price and can now begin a new life in a new home. The seller should feel that he received a fair market price and can now move on with his life elsewhere. Both sides are winners. Both the buyer and the seller can rejoice and celebrate at the closing.

Let's contrast that with the case outlined above where a relative is working on the details of a funeral with the director of the funeral home. He would expect to pay a fair and reasonable price, agree on some of the details and get out of there as quickly as possible.

In the same form and with the same solemnity you must view your divorce. You can hope all you want for the best-case scenario, but you would be well advised to prepare yourself for the realities of the divorce and set sensible and appropriate goals.

"Getting to OK" captures the essence of the goals that you should set for yourself. By "OK," I mean to say that you should strive for reasonable resolutions. Stay focused on reaching an agreement that allows you to survive with all your pieces in tact. You should hope and insist on being treated in a fair and reasonable manner during the process, neither expecting to be afforded any special treatment nor accepting any type of abuse from your adversaries. Most importantly, you should look forward to being able to quickly move on with your life once the proceedings are complete.

The following list includes some statements that should help you stay focused on the task at hand and shy away from overly aggressive expectations. In the spirit of "Getting to OK," they highlight reasonableness as opposed to competitiveness.

I hope …
• To finalize the divorce in a 'civil' manner.
• That I will be able to agree with my wife on most, or at least some, of the important issues that we face.
• That the final details of the divorce are decided upon in a fair and impartial way.
• That I am not taken advantage of.
• That the final divorce will fall within the average range of settlements for divorces that have the same attributes as my own.
• That by keeping my emotions in check, I can avoid getting hurt any further and stay away from saying or doing things that I will later regret.
• That I will be able to support myself financially during the divorce proceedings.
• That when the divorce is finalized, I will be in a position to move on with my life.
• To be able to reach an agreement or have a judgment rendered that allows me to maintain a reasonable standard of living after the divorce.

These goals are sensible and rational. Make them your own and dispense with overly aggressive or rigid stances, and you will be well on your way to finalizing an agreement that you and your ex-wife can live with.

The Court System

As you will bear witness to in the upcoming weeks and months, the court system is like no other organization in the world. If you have never been involved in a legal proceeding before, consider yourself blessed. You are in for a big surprise. The next section lays out some of the realities of the court system that I have experienced and that many other men in your situation confirmed.

Be Prepared to Wait!

I used to think that doctors and lawyers were the worst. They both had a tendency to schedule too many appointments in a day. Appointments would then overlap, leading to extended waiting times in the office. It seemed that no matter how early I would arrive at the office, I would wait an oppressively long time before I would be escorted inside.

This was before I got involved with our magnificent court system. Through my experience, I was taught the virtue of patience, or more accurately, I was forced to keep my mouth shut and bear it.

The fact is that there will be thousands of other divorce cases going on across the country at the same time as yours. The system is overloaded with cases.

The first issue that you will see is that it is extremely complicated to even schedule a court appearance. Dates and times have to be devised so that your lawyer, your wife's lawyer, your wife and yourself can all make the date and time. Then, the court must have an opening at that time. The court will then give a few dates that it currently has open. Telephone calls will go back and forth between all the parties involved to agree upon a date. If none of the dates are viable options, then calls have to be made to the courthouse once again and later dates are given. When a date is finally agreed upon, you should roughly expect that it will be between one and two months down the road. You may get lucky and be able to speed up the process a little, but on the whole, given the number of people that are involved in the case and taking into account their hectic schedules, finding a mutually acceptable date and time for everyone can be a Herculean task.

Now assume that a date has been chosen. You would think that the date would be set in stone and you mentally prepare yourself for the arrival of that fateful day. However, in almost all of the scheduled court appearances that were scheduled on my behalf, one thing or another caused the date to be adjusted. A lawyer might have a conflict with another case or with a personal matter that gets classified as an "emergency." This emergency overrides your time slot. Something might even come up in your own life that would make it impossible to get to court on that date. Perhaps a big meeting is scheduled at work that you simply cannot miss.

More likely, however, the court will decide to reschedule. The judge who handles your case is involved with many highly complex cases, all at the same time. If an issue arises in a case that requires immediate attention, he or she will reshuffle the schedule.

This is not an extraordinary event—it is standard operating procedure. The court will constantly review their schedule and the judge is not embarrassed to change a previously agreed upon date. In the courthouse, the judge makes the rules.

On your part, try to be as flexible as possible during this time and open up your calendar to accommodate the schedules of others. Once a date is agreed upon, be ready for it to be changed. As you get closer and closer to the date, chances are that it will stick. I recommend that you give a one minute call to your lawyer at least once a week to simply ask, "Am I still on for….?" Oftentimes, the lawyer hears from the court that a change was made but is too busy to contact you right away or simply forgets to let you know.

Now let's talk about the court date itself. Whether you are scheduled for a morning or afternoon appearance, be prepared for anything. It is possible that everything will go smoothly and that you can get in and out of the court with no problem. Chances are that something will happen to prolong the event. A lawyer may be delayed. The court is sympathetic to the plight of the lawyer. If a lawyer has not yet arrived, the judge will move on to the next case. When the lawyer does appear, his case will probably be heard next. Often, the cases that precede your own will simply take longer than expected. Verbal hearings can sometimes take much more time than anticipated and it is simply impossible to predict exactly when you will get your turn. Bottom line—you may find yourself waiting in a stuffy courtroom for hours at a time with nothing to do.

To combat this, prepare accordingly. If you are scheduled for a morning appointment, such as 9:00am or even 10:00am, make sure that your own schedule is clear the entire morning. Free up your calendar at work and tell your boss that you will arrive in the afternoon. If you have an afternoon appointment, do the same and see to it that your afternoon calendar is wide open. The best time for a court appearance would be late in the afternoon, such as 3:00 or 4:00. Most judges and court employees do not like to work late hours. After all the hearings of the day, they have enough paperwork that requires their attention, so they prefer to finish with the cases on hand as quickly as possible. If you have a late appointment, chances are that the judge will speed things along to make sure that the case is heard. Of course, there is always the risk that there will be no time for your case on that day and someone might ask for a postponement, but this is not likely since the court recognizes the difficulties of setting any date. If everyone is present, your case will probably be heard.

Second, always make sure that you have something to do while you wait in the courtroom. Bring along work that you can carry with you. Take a book that you would like to read for pleasure, or a newspaper or magazine. Use the time to work on your own case or think about what you will do in the next few days. Prepare a grocery list. Write a poem. Draw. It doesn't really matter what you do. The point is to have a pen handy and something to read or occupy yourself with while you wait for your case to go before the judge.

Third, take along something to eat and drink. You will need to replenish your energy after waiting so long in the courtroom. You do not want to run out of steam before your chance has even arrived. If your body is screaming for nourishment, you will feel weak and lethargic and will likely get a headache. Bring along some snacks, such as fruit, vegetables, energy bars or granola bars. If you feel tired, step outside the room, get some fresh air and have one of your snacks. Your body will thank you for it, and you will be able to think more clearly.

At times, men overestimate their strength or pretend that nothing bothers them. We view ourselves as tough and invincible, and we sometimes believe that nothing can get to us.

Despite all this, I have heard the same court experiences recounted over and over again by men who are getting divorced. These men found themselves sitting in a dry, depressing and humorless room. They sat impatiently and waited in fear. The judge has the power to dictate when and how you might see your children and how much of your hard-earned money will actually make its way to your own pocket. No matter how stalwart or muscle-bound you might be, the pressure under these conditions will mount and weigh heavily upon you.

It is not an easy thing for a man to be so helpless, and you must prepare yourself accordingly. To begin with, if you feel tense and uncomfortable, know that you are not alone. Most men before you have felt the same way, and it is only a natural reaction to the situation.

It is precisely at a time like this that you need to remind yourself how mentally strong you truly are and must be. Most people were never tested before in such a way and will be unaccustomed to the physical response to such stress. Your body will react in strange ways. Your adrenaline will begin to pump, and you may not feel like yourself. You may feel weak, faint or dizzy. Nevertheless, you do have the strength deep within you to make it through this time and keep in control of your own body.

Without sounding too feminine, there are a few things that you can do to help you relax. In court, it is helpful to utilize visualization, where you mentally transport yourself to a different state of being and visualize that you are somewhere else. This is used in meditation all the time, something you may have heard your mother, sister or wife talk about. I used to be very skeptical of this kind of talk.

The thing is-some relaxation and meditation techniques actually work. Let me translate this into a language that a man can understand: Picture yourself with a beer in your hand and no worries in the world. Feel relaxed? If you like, imagine that you are lying down on a soft and comfortable couch, watching your favorite sports team destroying a hated rival. How does this feel? Good? I think so too.

Imagining that you are in different places and states of mind will help you to relax and remain calm. Visualization can help you keep your cool when dealing with the court system, a time when you will need it most.

Next, and at the risk of sounding like your high-school gym teacher, take some deep breaths. Close your eyes, breathe in through your nose to a count of five, and breathe out slowly to a count of seven. Sounds silly? My apologies. Just do it anyway, and it will help you stay calm and put things in perspective.

Most importantly, and if at all possible, try to have someone close to you go along for the ride and keep you company in court.

I was fortunate to have the support of my family during the divorce process, and their help was invaluable to me. When I would go to court, my brother or mother would usually escort me and sit by my side. They were both very supportive, and their presence had a calming effect on me. I had someone to talk to, and this kept my mind off of everything that was going on around me. I don't know what I would have done without them.

Let me add a caveat to that. Having family members or close friends with you can also be a bit risky. Some people can make matters worse. They can rile you up, re-open old wounds or prove sympathetic to your wife. There are times when you will be better off alone. If you feel that your relatives can be inflammatory and add fuel to a raging fire, leave them home. If you have an inkling of fear that someone that you bring along will say something inappropriate or do something that will hurt your case, this fear can only add to your anxiety and do you harm. Tell them as diplomatically as you can that they cannot escort you to court. Then try to find someone whose presence would be helpful to you.

When I would go to court with someone, I would explicitly tell that person not to say anything or do anything—"Just stay with me and keep me company." I was lucky that I had such people on my side and I hope that you do as well. If no one is able to escort you to court, don't despair. This just means that you will have to work a little harder at being your own ally and giving yourself support. While the support of others is helpful, you still have the strength within you to persevere, even if it means going alone. You will need to become an expert at encouraging yourself and remaining in control of your emotions.

You are going through a major upheaval in your life. Oftentimes, under such circumstances, we tend to believe that the people around us understand what we are going through, empathize with us and actually care.

Let's get one thing straight about the type of individuals that you will encounter in court. To the court employees, your case represents nothing new. No matter how unique your case is, and believe me, it is the most important aspect of your life, the court employees have seen it all. Day in and day out, they see battling husbands and wives come and go. Many couples are civil; some are not. The crazy ones serve as topics of conversation for court employees at coffee or cigarette breaks. They shuffle mounds of paper from one office to another and file thousands of forms with tiny letters the size of grains of sand.

These workers are not inherently bad for being unsympathetic to your pain. The employees in court, including the clerks, bailiffs, legal secretaries and even the judges do this type of work for a living. It is hard to believe, I know, but for whatever reason, there are those that have chosen this line of work. What a life they must lead! They are running a business like any other business, and inventory moves in and out at a rapid rate. You are now part of the inventory and the job of the court system is to get you in, processed and out as quickly as they can. They do not want problems or "situations" on their hands. They just want you to leave as quickly as possible. They want you to agree on a settlement, and they do not necessarily care if it is a fair one. You surely would want to move the inventory as well if you worked in the divorce or family court system. It is your job and your attorney's job to protect your interests. Understand that despite the emotions that are inherently involved in this line of work, the court employees have a job to do and they want to get it done. How you feel is none of their concern.

Next, remember that the court clerks are overworked since the system is overloaded with divorce cases. They are also underpaid and earning less than many divorce court clients. Put these two elements together and you have the recipe for disaster. With relatively low base salaries and desks stacked high with forms, there is low incentive to care about the job. Couple this with the emotional tirades that they have to endure by the "out of control" husbands or wives and pure nastiness can emerge. Over time, some court workers have shut themselves off to the emotional aspects of the cases that they deal with and have decided to focus solely on the job that they were hired to do.

Speaking objectively and in hindsight, this is all very well and good and it seems to make sense. In the heat of battle, however, and with your life hanging in the balance, an apathetic or rude court clerk can set you off.

I remember the day that I had a scheduled court appearance. When I came to the courtroom, there was no one there. I tried to ask a few people who worked in the building what was going on, but they shrugged their shoulders and told me that they had no idea what I was talking about. Finally, I saw a familiar face from the courtroom; he was the man that called out the cases for the judge. I asked him what had happened. He looked at me curiously and said, "Are you telling me you don't know? Don't you people read anything? There is a sign on the wall over there, go read it! How many times …" He shook his head as he turned his back and walked away.

I was stunned. My instincts told me to take hold of this man's head and gouge his eyes out with my thumbs. I calculated the distance between his head and the nearest chair and I wondered if I could hit him with it. What could I do, though? He had the power in the courthouse. I had to suck it up and read the sign that I had missed. I was shaken for the entire day and I could not think straight. The scene ate at me inside for more than a month until I was able to forget it. I know now that I would have been better off just looking the other way and forgetting about the whole incident as quickly as possible.

You may meet some good people in court; some workers may be helpful at times. You must, however, recognize what you are facing and not arrive with the misguided notion that the workers are your friends or care about your welfare. So what should you do?

Recognize that the court employees have seen it all and cannot become personally involved with every case that they encounter. This will set the proper tone for you and help you steer clear of grandiose expectations.

Next, take on a serious and respectful tone with anyone that you come in contact with in court. Do not joke around and make small talk, unless you are sure that the person you are speaking with has initiated the conversation. Be polite and choose your words carefully. Do not, under any circumstances, insult the employee or raise your voice at him or her. Doing such a thing will only come back to haunt you. Humble yourself for the time being and ask your questions with sincerity. I would use the phrase, "I'm sorry to interrupt, but could I please ask you a question?" When I would ask questions in such a way, they would usually consider my request and provide an answer. Don't expect more than this and you will not be in for a shock, as I was.

Finally, if you are going to a courtroom that you have never been to before, leave yourself plenty of time to locate it. Call beforehand and get directions. Don't wait until the morning of the appearance to look it up on the internet. Leave yourself an hour to get through security and find your room. You need at least two visits to get a clear sense of how the building operates and exactly how much time you need to allow in the future. If you are early enough, you will be less sensitive to any uncooperative employees whom you may encounter.

Remember this rule: The Law Was Not Written for the "Good" Man!

The laws pertaining to divorce have evolved over time, and during this time, the courts have seen their fair share of dead-beat husbands and fathers. There have been so many cases of men who have shirked their responsibilities or the mandates of the court that many laws are now specifically designed to address these types of men and protect the women and children who are dependent upon them.

The good, responsible and honest husband will suffer because of this and find himself feeling that he is up against a long, uphill battle. Whether or not you are one of the ex-husbands or fathers who do not live up to their responsibilities is not at issue here. You are up against a court system that is wary of you. Throughout the proceedings, you may feel that the law is simply not fair and indeed, no one is claiming that it is. The question remains, "What does this mean to you?"

You are at an inherent disadvantage at the onset, but this should not translate into total dejection. Now is the time to focus on those areas that are under your control. Understand this: you will not be able to change the laws. You will not convince the judge that a law is ridiculous. Instead, you must learn to work within the framework of the law. You will need to educate yourself on what the law would dictate under various scenarios. Your lawyer might try to prove that a specific law is not applicable to your case, but again, once it is clear that the law does apply, it will not be within your control to change it.

What this really means for you is that for certain issues that you will face, you will be considered guilty until proven innocent. This does not mean that you are guilty, however; you will just have to do a better job at proving your innocence. You will have to document all of your actions and clearly demonstrate that you have done what you are claiming. The best way to do this is to provide factual, irrefutable documentation that backs up any assertions that you make.

Many of the protective measures that are in place deal with legal intervention intended to force you to take a specific action. For example, the court might use its power to take maintenance, child support or other payments directly from your salary and not give you the dignity of allowing you to make these payments on your own.

Let's examine the case of a wife who comes to court and asks the court to take the child support payments directly from the paycheck of her ex-husband. She claims that he is always late in making the payments and sometimes does not make the payments at all. If we were to stop right there and no additional evidence were offered, the court might accept her argument at face value and rule in favor of her request.

What would happen, however, if the husband walked into court with a journal log of all the payments that he has made? He shows the cancelled checks that his ex-wife has cashed and proves that not one payment was missed. He then proceeds to provide additional documentation as to the purchases that he has made on behalf of the children that are above and beyond the child support payments, such as clothing, shoes and money given for school trips. The court now has enough evidence to rule in his favor and deny the motion for payments to be taken directly from his salary.

I will expand upon the importance of documentation in the next chapter, but for the purposes of facing reality, you must recognize that you are up against all the dead-beats who have come before you and who have forced the court system to protect the women and children.

Don't expect universal fairness from the court. You are guilty until proven innocent, and because of this, you will have to do some convincing of your own before anyone will believe you. This is not impossible. While you can't change the laws, you certainly can offer documentation that proves your intention to be serious about fulfilling your duties and responsibilities.

In summary, here are some recommendations on how to deal with the court system that you are now a part of:

1. *Be prepared for the worst and free up your calendar for the entire morning or afternoon of every court date.*

2. *Bring along some work or reading material to keep yourself occupied.*

3. *Pack some snacks.*

4. *Stay calm, visualize that you are somewhere else and take plenty of deep breaths.*

5. *If at all possible, bring someone supportive and trustworthy to court with you.*

6. *Realize that the court employees deal with hundreds of cases and have seen it all.*

7. *If you are going to a courtroom for the first time, allow plenty of time to find your destination.*

8. *Don't expect total fairness. You are at a disadvantage because of some men who have come before you.*

9. *Through irrefutable documentation, you can prove to the court that you are serious about living up to your responsibilities.*

CHAPTER 3

▼

WHAT YOU CAN DO—
RIGHT NOW!

Now that you have begun to prepare yourself for some of the realities of the divorce proceedings, you may feel a sense of impending doom. Glancing back at the first section on "facing reality," I realize that the process might appear daunting. I wish that I were able to lighten it up a little bit, but then it would not be reality and I would be doing you a disservice. Many men, including myself, have felt besieged at the onset of the divorce and that is nothing to be ashamed of. Many of the items discussed in 'facing reality' dealt with realities that are outside your control. You cannot change the laws, the court system or the employees with whom you will interact.

Now it's time to focus your attention on what you can do *right now* to better position yourself for the upcoming proceedings. What information should you be collecting? How should you document your actions? What will you need to know about the law? Do you need to tell your boss or co-workers?

In the next section, these questions will be answered. You will find concrete measures that you should be taking today to help you get a grip on the situation. Here we will move away from the abstract and focus on those issues that *are* under your control and that you should be acting upon in the very near future.

Getting Organized

Throughout the divorce proceedings, you will be called upon to provide supporting documentation and third-party statements to back up any claims that you make. It will not be enough to state that you earn a certain salary or pay expenses if there is no proof. The court will only consider factual evidence and will not simply accept your word.

When a friend of mine named Billy was leaving his lawyer's office one day, the lawyer handed him a twenty-page document to fill out. It contained a slew of financial information that needed to be inputted, including Billy's salary, expenses, assets, liabilities and much more. And by the way, the lawyer needed it in two days, along with copies of all supporting statements.

Billy was at a loss for words. His records were in disarray. Statements were scattered around his apartment. How could Billy possibly fill out this financial worksheet? Where would he even begin? Now Billy was truly overwhelmed! Don't put yourself in that position. Do the following three things:

Start collecting all of the documentation that you have in all the corners of your own house and begin to organize them. Sort the statements into meaningful piles or folders and clearly label them. Knowing what you have and what you do not have is the first step.

Second, if you realize that you are missing information that will be required, start requesting the documentation from the sources right away. Banks, brokerage houses and payroll departments all have the capability of furnishing you with copies of previous statements. All you need to do is make the requests.

Lastly, if you have not been keeping adequate records up to this point, you must start today. No matter what, do not get discouraged at what you don't have right now. File away every letter and statement that you receive from this point forward and before you know it you will have accumulated a few months worth of most of the relevant documentation that will be required. Retain every bill and bank statement from this point on.

When *your* lawyer tells you to fill out financial worksheets or provide copies of bank statements, you should have everything at your fingertips. There should be no doubt as to what you have and what you do not have and you should be in a position to provide copies immediately or tell your lawyer that the statement is in the mail. Now is the time to get organized. Don't wait any longer, and save yourself the headaches later on.

Let's dig a little deeper into the documentation that you should begin to organize and collect. I have classified the relevant documentation into the following six categories:

1. **Income**

2. **Expenses**

3. **Assets**

4. **Liabilities**

5. **Lifestyle**

6. **Support**

For each category, you will find a list of standard documentation that will be required as back-up. The lists provided are not all-inclusive and you may find that you have specific circumstances that require additional statements.

Income

Your income will be vital in calculating any maintenance payments, child support payments or other payments that you may be required to make. In collecting support for your income, you should locate and organize the following:

- Tax returns for the last five years
- Supporting documentation for the tax returns, such as W-2 forms and interest & dividend statements
- Partnership income forms
- Pay stubs from your workplace for the past year
- Any rental income documentation that you claimed on your tax returns
- Sources of income not reported on your W-2 form, such as tips received
- Any other sources of income you may have

Expenses

Your expenses act as an offset to your income. While it is true that some payments are calculated based upon gross income alone, the court will usually take an overall "net" income approach or use an "ability to pay" approach when calculating other payments, such as maintenance, for example. For this reason, it is crucial that you organize your expense records and begin to track all of your expenses today.

In contrast to the information collected to support your income, your expenses go way beyond your tax returns. Remember that most day to day expenses are not tax deductible, but this does not mean that they do not affect your ability to make payments or your overall net income. In addition, the expenses that you claim need not be totally supported by documentation. While some expenses are clearly supported by statements, such as mortgage payments or car insurance payments, more commonplace expenses might be made with cash, such as meals or transportation. These too constitute expenses, and you should track them. For such expenses, the court will expect a certain degree of reasonableness, but the fact that an expense was paid for in cash should not preclude you from acknowledging it. The greatest risk lies in not reporting expenses that you actually incur because you either forget about them or do not think that they are important. Every expense adds up, so it pays to list them. Don't shortchange yourself.

When listing your expenses, keep in mind the following items:

- Mortgage payments or rental payments
- Co-op or condo maintenance payments
- Tax bills, including real-estate taxes
- Credit card bills for the past two years—to help support the expenses paid for by credit card
- Medical expenses, including medical insurance, doctor co-payments and prescription medicines
- Telephone bills
- Cell-phone bills
- Electric bills
- Gas bills
- Cable or satellite dish bills
- Legal bills (You probably have made payments to your lawyer and will continue to do so in the near future.)
- Clothing, suits, jackets and shoes purchases

- Eyewear expenses, including glasses and contact lenses
- Car insurance payments
- Car upkeep payments, including oil changes, tune-ups, inspections, and any major repairs expensed during the past two years
- Gas for your car
- AAA membership dues
- Membership dues to professional associations
- Groceries
- Drinks and snacks
- Dining out
- Daily meals
- Vacations
- Entertainment expenses, including trips to the movies, theater, museums, or shows for the children
- Toiletries, such as soap and shampoo
- Computer related expenses, such as hardware repairs and purchases of paper, toner and ink
- Commuting expenses, such as subway, railroad and parking expenses
- Internet service bills
- Purchases of books and magazines for work, school or pleasure
- Educational expenses, including tuition, books and supplies
- Furniture for a new residence
- Apartment upkeep, such as vacuum cleaner, cleaning material and plumbing, electric and roof repairs
- Donations to charity
- Membership dues to religious associations, such as a Church or Synagogue

Assets

In addition to your income, your current assets play a role in determining your ability to make certain payments as well as establishing your overall level of wealth. It will also be important to understand what your assets are since there will undoubtedly be some determinations made as to the allocation of these assets to you and your wife. Listing your assets now will not only help you quickly fill out financial worksheets, but it will also force you to start thinking about the assets that you would like to keep at the conclusion of the divorce.

When collecting information on your assets, keep the following items in mind:

- Real estate property, such as homes or buildings
- Mortgage documentation on any real estate
- Appraisal reports showing the current market value of real estate
- Car or boat titles
- Bank account balances, including savings and checking accounts for the prior year
- Pensions and 401K statements from your workplace
- Life Insurance policies, with statements reflecting the current cash value of the policies
- Stocks & bonds investment holdings, including brokerage statements
- Profit-sharing pension plan balances
- Stock option holdings
- Valuable jewelry or gold and silver
- Home furniture, including bedroom sets, dining room sets, kitchenware and rugs
- Professional licenses, such as a law degree, medical degree or CPA (Yes, these licenses are considered assets and will play a role in the divorce proceedings.)

Liabilities

In the same way that your expenses act as an offset to your income, your current liabilities act as an offset to your assets. Taken together, your combined assets and liabilities represent your true "net" assets or your level of wealth. Since the court will take your liabilities into account, it is important that you provide information on all of your outstanding liabilities. Some of these liabilities will overlap with the expenses that you have listed, but in general, your expenses represent more routine payments while liabilities are more long-term in nature.

When listing your liabilities, remember to include the following:

- Mortgage balances on any real estate
- Student loans under your name that are due or coming due
- Annual life-insurance premium payments
- Outstanding loans from major lenders
- Substantial outstanding credit card bills
- Loans from family members or friends (cancelled checks or notarized statements can attest to these)
- Legal bills (outstanding legal bills related to the divorce will eventually have to be paid, so they do represent a liability)
- Principal balances on car or boat loans
- Loans taken out against your pension plan or 401K plan at work

Lifestyle

The concept of "lifestyle" relates to the standard of living that the husband or wife was accustomed to during the marriage. Generally speaking, the court prefers that the lifestyle that was maintained during the marriage should be sustained after the marriage has dissolved. In some cases, one spouse will paint a picture of a lavish lifestyle and argue that a specific sum of money is required to maintain such a lifestyle.

I mention this concept here so that as you gather all the documentation above, you keep in mind the type of picture that you would like to paint of yourself to the court. You will need to ask yourself the following questions, "What type of lifestyle was my wife truly accustomed to? What documentation can be used to either support a lifestyle argument by me or refute a lifestyle argument put forward by her?"

Understanding the concept of "lifestyle" will help you gather the information that might one day be used as supporting evidence for your side of the story. The documentation that relates to lifestyle will overlap with the items listed in the income, expenses and assets sections above. Unlike the documentation above, however, which focused more on your own income and expenses, documentation relating to 'lifestyle' relates primarily to the expenses that were incurred jointly by you and your wife throughout the entire marriage or at least during the past few years.

The fact that you and your wife took a two-week cruise last year does not prove much. It could have been the first vacation that you took in ten years. On the other hand, it could have been one of the five vacations that you and your wife have been taking consistently every year for the past five years.

For the purposes of a "lifestyle" argument, the following items should be of particular relevance to you:

- Tax returns for a number of years, demonstrating prior income levels for a span of time

- Credit card bills that support or refute claims of exorbitant purchases for expensive clothing or jewelry

- Expenses incurred for vacations, or lack thereof

- Entertainment expenses such as movies, expensive dinners and Broadway shows, or lack thereof

- Types of homes lived in and cars driven over the past few years

- Life insurance policies purchased over the past few years

- Investment holdings purchased over the past few years

- Level of common home expenses, such as gas, electric and telephone bills, which could signal extravagance or conservatism

- Cancelled checks of gifts for weddings, bar mitzvahs, etc.

- Charitable donations made over the past few years

Support

From the time that the divorce proceedings begin until the time that the final divorce decree is granted, chances are that you will find yourself living in separate quarters from your wife and incurring your own expenses. You may still make payments in support of your wife or your children, if you have any. This may include paying the mortgage or rent, paying living expenses such as the gas and electric bills, and even making payments to purchase necessities for the children, such as food and clothing.

I want to stress the importance of keeping track of these payments and documenting them. You may one day need to prove that although you were separated, you continued to support your wife and the children, and this can certainly go a long way in either supporting your own claims or refuting any assertions made by your wife of you 'abandoning' your family.

First, make sure that you make such payments by check and not by cash. If you pay cash, you will have no documentation. Second, when paying a bill on behalf of your wife, request the bill itself or at least a copy of the bill. Make sure that you mail the bill yourself and look for the cancelled check in your next bank statement. You should not tell your wife that you do not trust her; simply state that you would like to maintain the proper records and receipts.

The following items are of specific relevance in regards to support:

- Cancelled checks of any payments made to your wife

- Statements of expenses and cancelled checks for any bills that were paid on behalf of your wife

- Documentation that supports any expenses incurred on behalf of the children, such as purchases of clothing, food or entertainment

- Any medical bills paid on behalf of your wife or children

Keeping a Journal

So far, we have only talked about "getting organized" in terms of financial data and external, supporting statements. However, you will be called upon to provide personal information about yourself and your entire family. You will also be asked to provide a chronology of events, starting from the time that you met your wife and got married to the current date.

This might sound like an easy thing to do, but providing such a chronology requires much thought. Recalling everything that happened between you and your wife that led up to the divorce, by sheer memory alone, will be virtually impossible.

More importantly, many events are about to take place that you will be required to relay back to your lawyer or a judge, and relying upon your memory could prove to be a grave mistake. We tend to believe that we never forget anything. Yet, we are human. Time goes by, and we can easily forget dates or times or comments made. The past becomes hazy and blurry, especially under duress. *Bottom line*—you cannot rely on your recollection alone at a time like this.

My advice to you is this—***start preparing and writing things down today!*** Don't wait until you are face to face with a divorce attorney to start thinking about chronologies and dates. Begin to prepare yourself right now, from the point that you realize that divorce is a realistic possibility, and you will spare yourself a tremendous amount of anxiety and worry in the near future.

The first step is to purchase a journal. Any standard spiral notebook or hardcover, black & white notebook will do. It does not have to be fancy or extravagant.

The second step is to start thinking about and writing down some personal information and a chronology of events of your relationship with your wife. You will need this information at some point, so now would be a good time to see what you remember and identify what you need to research. You may not remember everything today, but you can fill in the blanks as you remember more and as you check your records and speak with other people.

Here is a list of topics that you should have at your fingertips. Open up your journal and designate the first few pages to jotting down personal information and events that have occurred in the past.

- All ages and dates of birth, including those of your wife and any children of the marriage

- Social Security Numbers, including your own, your wife's and any children

- Places of residence that you and your wife lived throughout the marriage

- Levels of education and schools attended, including your own, your wife's and any children

- Religious affiliations of the family

- Your profession and your wife's profession

- Employment history for you and your wife, including employer names and locations

- Where and how you met your wife

- The date of the marriage and how long you were married

- Your relationship with your wife and children (Were there good times? Bad times? Abuse?)

- What type of lifestyle did you have? Did you take expensive vacations? Drive an expensive car?

- How close are you with your children?

- If you are currently living apart, how did this come about?

- For how long have you been separated?

- Does anyone in the family have medical problems?

- Does anyone in the family have addictions, such as drug, alcohol or gambling problems?

- Why are you getting divorced—at least in your mind?

- What specific events have led up to this point?

- Do you and your wife agree to the divorce, or is one party alone driving the process?

- A general chronology of events from the time that you were married to the time that you realized that a divorce was imminent

- A chronology of important events from the time that you realized that a divorce was imminent to the current date

- How do you feel about the divorce?

- Did you seek marriage counseling or help from clergy to work on saving the marriage?

Write down as much as you can and start looking up any information that you are not certain of. Tax returns might help you with ages and social security numbers. Cancelled checks can help you remember when and how many times you visited a marriage counselor. Your lawyer will certainly want to know as much about the case as possible when advising you about your options.

The third and most important step is to utilize the journal as a tool for documenting important events that happen from this point forward. I hope that you should never have to call upon the journal in a court of law, but if you should ever have to, you will be glad that you have been documenting.

You will need to include factual information in motions that you make to the court, and your lawyer will look to you to give dates and facts as to what happened at various times. Don't rely on your memory.

The specific circumstances of every divorce case are unique and I cannot tell you exactly what you have to document. There are, however, some general topics that will eventually emerge in most divorce cases, and keeping these in mind will help you determine what you should begin to keep track of.

Let's take the case of a father who loved his children dearly and who wants to continue to have a relationship with them after the divorce. The wife has a right to claim anything that her heart desires. What you need to do is document events that would support your assertions about your current relationship with the children. As examples, this would include how much time you spend with them, what you do with them, the types of places that you take them, the food that you prepare for them … Anything that you are doing that can help you back up your claims down the road should be documented. Perhaps the issue never arises during the divorce and you are satisfied with the final resolution. In that case, you can burn the journal at your next barbecue. If, however, claims are made about you and your relationship with your children that are false, a documented history of the relationship will come in handy.

Now, let's face facts; at times there is a terribly ugly side to divorce. Not every divorce is civilized and peaceful. Hurtful things are said and done. Property mysteriously disappears. Threats are made. Sometimes your wife will be to blame and sometimes you will be to blame. You need to document everything that is happening. If your wife says something to you that is relevant to the divorce, write it down because you may have to remember it later on. If a threat is made, document it. If you speak to your wife on the phone and it turns nasty, document the nature and substance of the conversation. Dates and facts will be vital to you in the future.

Use your common sense and make a determination as to what is important and what is not. Any actions that will help support an assertion of yours, such as your devotion to your children or your unwillingness to get involved in a verbal duel with your wife or her family should be documented. Any event that plays a role in the divorce, such as a threatening statement, the changing of locks or the disappearance of your own personal property must be documented.

Doing this should take you about *five to ten minutes a day*. You do not have to write a novel. Just write down the facts that are important to the divorce. Here is an example of a potential entry in your journal:

Thursday—5/15/03

Talked to Jane and agreed that I would pick up the kids from school and take them to dinner.
Picked up Mike and Rebecca from school and took them to China Hunan. Had a great time. Dropped off the kids at 8:00.
Gave Jane a check for child support. Picked up the rent bill and the electric.

Educate Yourself

I hope that by this time you are beginning to view your divorce as a business transaction in which you are deeply involved. It has great importance in your life, but it is a transaction nonetheless, and it must be given at least the same amount of value and effort as any other undertaking that you embark upon. It is in your best interest to get involved with the process as early as possible and learn as much as you can.

It is fair to say that you will not become an expert in divorce proceedings right now. You will not be able to know the laws pertaining to divorce for all fifty states. Don't start out on your quest by thinking that you must accomplish these impossible tasks. To do so would take years of schooling, training and experience, and even the most seasoned divorce attorneys must do their fair share of research as new issues arise and as the laws continue to evolve.

What you *should* do right now, however, is begin to familiarize yourself with the issues that are involved in a divorce and the laws that might apply to your case. Your goal here is not to give professional advice to others, but rather to give yourself a taste of what must ultimately be resolved and a sense of how the court will rule on various issues in the jurisdiction where you live. With this knowledge, you can play an active role in the divorce proceedings, rather than be a passive bystander. You will be in a position to ask meaningful and thoughtful questions to your lawyer and be a part of the strategic aspects of your case, and also understand the various options that your lawyer will offer you.

There are two general avenues that can be used to glean the information that you are searching for, each with its own benefits and drawbacks.

The first is word of mouth. There is a wealth of information that you can extract from friends or relatives who have gone through divorce. Some had positive experiences while others had dreadful ones. A friend of yours might even be a divorce attorney. By talking to these people, you will hear their stories and gain insight into the process.

The risk, however, is that many people embellish upon their own situations and present their case in a biased way. It is not their fault; this is simply human nature. Your job is to listen as much as possible, learn what you can, and then take the questions that you have back to an objective source, such as your own lawyer. Don't worry if you do not have a lawyer yet, just write down your questions and make sure to raise them later on.

The point here is to listen carefully but to take the stories of others with a grain of salt. You can certainly learn a tremendous amount by talking to others, but keep in mind that each person has only one point of view. Just listen, ask questions if you want to understand better, and save the critique for when you speak to someone more knowledgeable.

Take the case of Anthony who was in the initial stages of a divorce. He had two children whom he loved dearly. His friend from work, an Iranian named Kamal, heard about Anthony's situation and told him one day by the water cooler that he might as well kiss his children goodbye. The laws in America were totally unfair. The father has no rights and the courts walk all over them. He said that the mother will certainly get custody, and he will be lucky if he even gets visitation. Kamal casually walked back to his desk, not noticing or caring about the look of terror on Anthony's face.

Everyone has his or her own perspective, and Kamal's was certainly influenced by his Iranian background. Kamal was accustomed to a world where the father rules the family and where custody of the children goes to the father once the child has reached a certain age. He did not like the concept of visitation and did not appreciate the fact that the court would dictate when and how he would see his children. He was bitter and angry at the system and exaggerated his own predicament. Anthony, on the other hand, was not familiar yet with the workings of the system and was thrown into a state of panic.

Instead of panicking, remember that everyone has a particular frame of reference, and oftentimes, stories are embellished. Anthony would have been the wiser if he listened to the story, empathized with Kamal and resolved to find out more about the issue of child custody. It does not really make logical sense that a father would be denied the opportunity to see his children under relatively normal circumstances. Could Kamal's story really apply to all cases? Anthony should have taken away some interesting points from the conversation but gone to his lawyer or a more knowledgeable source to answer the following questions:

- Is there a chance that I might not get to see my children?
- How is custody determined in this state?
- How are custody issues decided in most cases?

Despite the horror stories that exist, I still believe that there is much to learn by speaking to others and using common sense to determine what is applicable to you and what is not. Learn what you can by speaking to others who have divorce experience, but corroborate any relevant information with a knowledgeable source before you begin to panic.

By adopting a critical lens to view all that you see and hear, you will get a good sense of the issues that are involved and those that you should be wary of. Formulate questions from these discussions and either confirm their validity or prove their falsehood later on.

Another general source of information would be the literature that is at your disposal. Information on divorce can be found in either hard-copy format or through search engines on the internet. A visit to your local library will give you loads of information relating to divorce laws and cases. Alternatively, a search on the internet can provide you with anything from the written divorce laws for a multitude of issues that apply to your specific state to stories of divorce and survival by people who have gone through the process. Gathering this information can be useful to you, but here too, there are a number of drawbacks that you should be aware of.

First off, as you begin your search, you may feel overloaded. The librarian might recommend thirty-five books that apply to you, or you could browse through an internet search engine and find that there are two million matches. Don't worry so much or feel that you have to read all of this material. Your job right now is to get a sense of the issues and not to become an expert. Pick three sources of information and start there. Try to be specific in your choices, and focus on your state and issues that apply to you. If you do not have children, don't spend your time learning about custody and child support. If you live in Los Angeles, don't waste your time reading about changes to the laws in New York. Focus your research and begin to document the questions that you have and the areas of law that must be confirmed.

A second drawback of using hard-copy material and the internet is that in many cases, no matter how much research you do, the resolution is not always black or white. The information could very well be outdated, and more recent laws might have superseded a law that you have just read about. Even internet sites are not updated daily, and the information might be dated. Keep this in mind and do not make the assumption that any rule that you read about on the web is set in stone.

Alternatively, there might be a law that has not changed in terms of its wording, but its applicability in practice might have evolved over time through the court system. Even if you were to become familiar with all the laws of divorce, you would still not be able to determine how they are applied in practice under real case scenarios.

Finally, stories abound on the internet, and the same caveat that applies to the stories of your friends applies equally here. Feel free to read about the experiences of others, but recognize that each person comes from a distinct perspective and bias. Make sure not to panic if you read a story that frightens you. Pose questions later on to a knowledgeable source. Just because something is written in black and white does not mean that it is true.

Despite all of the drawbacks, it is still important for you to do some research. You need to acquire a certain degree of knowledge so that you can hold meaningful conversations with your lawyer. You need to prepare questions that will confirm or invalidate information that you found. And most importantly, you need to stay involved in the process and not pass the ball off to your lawyer. This will help you get a better sense of control during this uncertain time in your life.

I have touched upon the fact that you will be seeking to confirm information through a knowledgeable source, such as your lawyer. Let's add another element to the mix. Whoever your lawyer is, he or she also comes with a suitcase of experiences and a specific perspective that has developed over many years. Your lawyer may be highly experienced, but at times, such experience can close a person off to new ideas and fresh outlooks. If the lawyer has suggested resolutions in the past that have failed, he or she might feel that there is no point in raising those options today, when in reality, such options could offer the perfect solutions to your problems.

You can provide that fresh perspective and complement the expert opinion of your lawyer with your own ideas. By having a working knowledge of the laws, you can ask questions that stimulate your lawyer's creative senses and help resolve complex issues. You could raise issues that your lawyer might not have thought about and that actually do apply to your case. You may have some skills of your own, such as financial analysis expertise, that you can apply to the case.

In short, you and your lawyer are partners, each with strengths and weaknesses. Your lawyer will want to learn as much about you as possible when he or she advises you in the case; in turn, you will need to learn as much as you can about the law so that you too have a sense of where your lawyer is coming from.

By merging these two distinct perspectives together, you both will formulate a plan and a strategy that is right for you.

Choose Wisely—Getting a Lawyer That's Right for You

Even if you are at the early stages of making the decision of getting a divorce, there is no reason to procrastinate about choosing a lawyer that is right for you.

Many people feel that they'll get one when they really need one. That is a terrible time for you to be choosing a lawyer. You do not want to have time pressures and outstanding motions weighing on your head when you sit down with a divorce attorney to explain your situation. You will be at a significant disadvantage if you find yourself trying to find a lawyer while the proceedings have taken on momentum of their own. You might rush into making a decision that proves in the final analysis to be misguided and costly.

Instead, start the process now. You will find that most divorce attorneys offer a free consultation. They will typically be willing to sit down with you, gain an understanding of your case and possibly offer some options and scenarios as to future outcomes, from best-case scenarios to worst case scenarios based upon their experience.

You can begin to take advantage of these free consultations with the objective of choosing a lawyer who will suit your needs if and when the time comes. While the lawyer will undoubtedly try to learn as much as he or she can about your case, you must take the opportunity to learn as much about the attorney as you can.

Don't just sit in the chair and answer the questions that are asked; ask your own questions and take notes so that you can compare the answers later on with the answers of other attorneys that you have spoken with. Remember, this is a two-way interview, so be pro-active and vocal in the conversation.

The lawyer is trying to determine if the case is worth his or her time and effort. Some lawyers only take specific types of cases, such as those that are high-profile, will generate a certain amount of revenues or possibly present a complex issue that can be the basis of a future publication in a legal journal. Let the lawyer worry about those issues; you must explain your case, and if the lawyer is not interested in taking it, say "thank you very much for your time" and go to someone else.

You, on the other hand, are trying to feel out the attorney and figure out whether or not you believe he or she is right for you. Here are some general concerns that you should look to address and some questions that you should have answered before you make any final decisions about hiring a lawyer.

1) Experience with Divorce Cases

If you are already sitting down with a divorce attorney, there is a good chance that the attorney specializes in divorce cases. This is not always the case, however. Some lawyers take on all types of cases and handle a slew of legal issues, from real-estate law to corporate tax law to personal injury.

In your situation, I recommend that you find a firm or an attorney who specializes in divorce and family law. In many cases, a law firm will have specialists in many areas, so even if a firm is not well known for divorce cases, it might have some individuals who focus on divorce and who have years of experience with such cases. That is perfectly fine. The goal is to be confident that the person representing you has the experience and knowledge that is required to competently handle your case and that this lawyer is supported by a strong firm.

On that note, don't take anything for granted and be assured that you have the right to ask questions regarding the attorney's experience. After the consultation, you should know the answers to the following questions:

- For how many years has the lawyer practiced law?

- Does he or she specialize in divorce cases?

- What percentage of time was spent on divorce cases in the past five years?

- Do any specifics of your case represent a complexity that the lawyer feels he or she may not be prepared to handle? (Few would admit to it, so you may have to decide this on your own!)

- How many other lawyers in the firm are knowledgeable in divorce cases and do the partners discuss the cases jointly to determine the best strategies?

- How many other lawyers in the firm specialize in divorce?

2) Does the Lawyer Have the Time?

You may believe that you have found the greatest lawyer imaginable. He or she may be an expert in the field and a perfect match for your case. The problem is, however, that because the lawyer is so great, your case could be insignificant and of no consequence to him or her.

What good will such expertise do for you? How will it help you to know that your lawyer is a star when you can't get in touch with him or her for an entire week?

This may not be the fault of the lawyer at all. Having many cases means that the lawyer is in high demand. Unfortunately, it might also mean that you will not be given the attention that you need and the care that your case requires. The lawyer may have the best of intentions, but there are only a certain number of hours in a day and only seven days in a week. Miracles are not going to happen. If your lawyer is overworked, he or she will not be able to focus on you.

Now is the time to find out just how accessible your lawyer is. You may not be able to get a direct answer today and few lawyers will flatly admit that they do not have time for you (although such an honest statement would be in the lawyer's as well as your own best interest). In addition, circumstances might change in the future and a once accessible attorney could evolve into a missing person. But today, you can get a sense as to how seriously the lawyer will take your case. By asking some tough questions now, you might help the lawyer realize that he or she really does not have the ability to take on your case, and possibly he or she can recommend you to a colleague of theirs.

Ask the following types of questions to determine your lawyer's accessibility:

- How many cases are you working on right now?

- Do you in any way feel that my case is so complex that you do not have the time to spend on it, given the other cases you handle?

- When would we typically meet? Mornings? Evenings? Are you flexible when meeting with clients?

- If I call the office with a question or concern, how long should I anticipate waiting before receiving a response?

- If your office receives a letter from the opposing attorney or a copy of a submitted court document, how long will it take your office to inform me?

- How many mornings or afternoons do you spend in court on your outstanding cases during a typical workweek?

- Do you have any scheduled vacations in the immediate future?

- If you were to go on vacation or get sick, is there someone in the office who could cover for you?

- With regards to this cover person, how often will he or she be briefed on my case? Is this person as knowledgeable as you are?

There are no right or wrong answers to these questions. Yet, by comparing the responses of a few lawyers, you can gauge who will be able to handle your case and who does not have the time to do so.

After interviewing a few lawyers, patterns will emerge that represent standards and benchmarks, and those lawyers whose responses are way off the chart, either in terms of too many cases handled or in terms of too few divorce cases currently being worked on should be removed from your list of candidates.

3) How Much Will This Cost Me?

Let's talk dollars and cents. You will need to take a careful look at how much of your savings you can allocate to the divorce. A divorce can cost from a few thousand dollars to possibly tens or hundreds of thousands of dollars, depending on the complexity of the case, the number of issues involved and the willingness of the parties to work together. As you discuss your case with prospective lawyers, make sure that you walk away with a good understanding of what you face in the coming weeks and months in terms of cost.

Because of the nature of every divorce case, it will be impossible for a lawyer to tell you how much your divorce will cost. The decisions that you make and the type of strategy that you choose will be a driving force as to the amount of time that your lawyer has to spend on the case. An even more important factor, however, which is out of your control, is the strategy adopted by your wife. It takes two to tango, and despite any ideas that you may have about civility, your wife may have other plans. You may find that your lawyer must work overtime to respond to motions made by your wife. How can anyone know what the bill will be?

Despite the uncertainty involved, there are some things that you can learn today that will help you in your decision process. While total costs are hard to estimate, hourly costs must be clearly specified in a retainer agreement (your initial agreement with your lawyer to have him or her represent you). In addition, based upon the facts of the case as you lay them out, attorneys can give you a sense of the time it will take to finalize the divorce under various scenarios. You can begin to develop a range of costs that you will incur and use this range to compare and contrast the lawyers you speak with.

Know the answers to the following questions related to cost before you leave the office:

- What is the hourly rate?

- Does the lawyer have any 'discounted' rates that you may be eligible for?

- How much money will it cost to retain the lawyer? This can range considerably depending on the lawyer and the complexity of the case. (Any unused fees are returned to you.)

- How must you pay the bills? Can a payment plan be worked out?

- In general, and based upon the facts as you have presented them, how much will the divorce ultimately cost?

While cost should not be the only factor, it is an important one. Your divorce is a big part of your life, but it may not be worth it to go into debt for the next twenty years as a result of it. Take a close look at the fee structures of the different lawyers and take the cost into account when making your final decision. I would not suggest that you choose a lawyer simply because he or she is the cheapest. It is possible, however, that some lawyers are simply not within your reach right now. If there is absolutely no way that you will be able to pay the fee or get the money for the retainer agreement, that lawyer is not right for you. Keep looking for a lawyer who is adequate but also affordable or at least flexible in terms of payment plans.

Many attorneys will work with you and help you spread your costs while they themselves still continue to generate revenues but collect the cash at a slower pace. You may be happily surprised to learn that a lawyer you would like to retain is willing to work out a payment plan as part of the final divorce settlement.

Don't make any assumptions that might lead you to either hire an inappropriate attorney or discard an attorney who would have been willing to work with you and within your budget. Ask the questions now and understand what you are getting into. The key point is to get everything out in the open so that there are no surprises down the road. Be firm in your desire to understand how much the divorce will cost. If a lawyer tries to change the subject or sidestep the issue, insist that your questions be answered. You have every right to ask these questions and you cannot make a decision without knowing the answers.

4) Does it 'Feel' Right?

You've asked the questions and gathered some information. Now it's time to think about the personal connection that you felt with each lawyer. Don't underestimate your gut feeling. You may want to reject an attorney who just did not seem genuine to you or who somehow rubbed you the wrong way.

Some people do not get along. This is not a reflection on either person; it is just a fact. It is possible that you just don't like an attorney. There are plenty of other lawyers out there, so you should never feel that you have to retain a specific one. If the lawyer is hitting you with an aggressive sales pitch, there's a good chance that he or she is desperate for clients and may not be what you are looking for.

After holding conversations with the prospective lawyers, think about the following questions:

- Did you feel comfortable with the lawyer?
- Did the lawyer help to ease some of your fears while still explaining the facts and realities of the case?
- Was the lawyer pleasant to deal with?
- Did the lawyer present professionalism?
- Did the lawyer ever lose his or her temper?
- Did you like the lawyer?

The lawyer does not have to be your best friend. Don't think that he or she will provide you with a shoulder to cry on. On the other hand, you will be spending a considerable amount of time with this person should you choose to use his or her services. At a minimum, you need to make sure that the lawyer is someone whom you will feel comfortable speaking with and working with. The lawyer is your partner, and just as you would only choose a partner that you feel secure with, so too should you choose your lawyer.

There is an important factor that you should look for relating to this topic. When you meet with the lawyer, pay close attention to what the lawyer asks and how he or she asks it. In general, there will be many decisions that you will need to make during the divorce proceedings, and you must understand that the decisions are **yours** to make, not the lawyer's. The lawyer can advise you about your options. He or she should explain what the resolution is likely to be under different scenarios. However, the lawyer should not force you into a course of action that you do not wish to take.

With this in mind, a lawyer that understands this concept will ask you these questions:

- What do you want to get out of the divorce?

- How important is it that you keep certain properties ... see your kids regularly ...?

- What is most important to you?

In later chapters we will discuss how you can answer some of these questions, but for now, it is important that the lawyer is asking them and is genuinely concerned with your responses. This is a good indicator that the lawyer will fight for your wishes and desires and not push you into making decisions for the sake of winning a legal argument.

Alternatively, imagine that a lawyer hears a little about your case and then tells you exactly what you have to do. He or she tells you that you must fight for custody, keep the house, and not pay any alimony. "I'll have a motion written up by next Tuesday ...," this lawyer might say.

A response like that would very well signify that the lawyer is not listening to you and will act according to his or her own agenda. Such a lawyer will do more harm than good.

Remember, the lawyer is there to help you get *what you want* and advise you on the best course of action. You need to have a lawyer by your side who will look out for your interests above all else.

Now that you have gathered information on the experience of the lawyers, the associated costs of each, and your relative comfort level with them, you can make an informed decision.

If it is still not time to hire the lawyer, you can rest assured that when the time does come, you will be prepared to retain proper representation quickly. If this is the case, let the lawyers know that you are not ready, but if and when the process advances, you will give them a call.

Let's recap the benefits that you have gained by doing your research now:

1. You have one less thing to worry about, and you can rest assured that you will not be forced into a bad decision.

2. You have developed a relationship with the attorney.

3. You have a list of lawyers that you can call upon. If your first choice is unable to take the case, you can move on to your second choice.

4. You have gained a better understanding of your own case and a sense of what your options are.

Don't Be Afraid to Walk Away

One final note before we move on. It is certainly possible that after you have selected a lawyer and paid the retainer fee, you find that you have made a grave mistake.

Perhaps the lawyer is not as accessible as you had hoped for. Conceivably, the lawyer may take on more cases after accepting your own and not give you the time anymore that you and your case require. You may realize that the lawyer is not well versed on some issues or gives unsound advice. Your feelings of comfort might change over time as you work with the lawyer on a day-to-day basis.

If you truly feel that the lawyer is doing an inadequate job and that he or she is not representing your best interests, don't hesitate to walk away. It is within your legal rights to tell the lawyer that the arrangement is not working out and that you will seek counsel elsewhere. That being said, the decision is one that must be weighed carefully.

I recommend that before you actually relieve the lawyer of his or her duties, you should speak to some other lawyers first and make sure that there is someone available to take on your case. You will need to weigh the benefits of getting a new lawyer at this stage of the game against the costs involved in leaving your current one. If, however, your lawyer is simply unbearable and doing such an abysmal job that you are better off without him or her, you might be more inclined to leave that lawyer and find someone else. If you find that you have nowhere else to go and that there is no possible way that you will be able to secure a new attorney quickly, you could decide to stick with your current one and become more active in the process yourself to compensate for the lawyer's ineptitude.

You do have a choice, and you should not feel that you are stuck with an attorney once you have signed a retainer agreement. With regards to any remaining balance of your retainer fee, the lawyer is legally bound to return this to you and provide a detailed billing statement that outlines all reductions to the retainer that were made. So if the necessity arises, know that you have the legal right to seek help elsewhere and don't hesitate to do so.

Informing Your Boss

When I discussed some of the realities of the court system, I touched upon the issue of time constraints and scheduled appointments. During the divorce proceedings, you will be called upon to spend time discussing your case with your lawyer, gathering financial and personal information and also going to court on many occasions. Now is the time to take a close look at how this new aspect of your life will affect your work environment.

If you are self-employed, you are very lucky. You have the ability to schedule appointments around the divorce proceedings and work extra hard after normal business hours to make up for time lost during the standard workday. Although this too will take perseverance and dedication on your part, you are at least in a position to make your own schedule and be the master of your time.

Most of us, however, are employees of large corporations or small businesses. If this is the case, ask yourself these questions:

- When and how will I be able to meet my lawyer or go to court?

- Will my boss allow me to take time off?

- Who should I inform about the divorce?

Think about your current position and responsibilities. It may be too early in the process to start informing others about the divorce, but you should begin to formulate a game-plan of how you will approach the workplace if and when the divorce begins to impose constraints on your time.

When I went through my divorce, I was fortunate enough to have a boss who was fair and understanding. I knew that he cared primarily about results and employee effort and attitude; he was not too picky about the exact hours that an employee might work or whether or not his employees worked from nine to five or from eight to four. In short, he was reasonable and flexible, and he was not interested in "face time". Knowing this, I was able to approach him and discuss the situation early on in the process. I wanted to accomplish the following by speaking directly with him:

1. Let him know that I am in the process of getting a divorce

2. Inform him that I will be required to spend some time either with my lawyer or in court

3. Ask him for some flexibility in the coming months with regard to my work schedule and the hours that I am in the office

4. Ensure him that despite the divorce, I take my work seriously and will do all in my power to make up for lost time, including working at night and on weekends, if required

5. Guarantee that as soon as I know of a scheduled appointment, I will let him know so that we can plan accordingly

By explaining the situation up front I was able to ease any fears that my boss may have had about the time that I would need. The key here is to ask for flexibility while demonstrating that you will do your part to make up for any lost time.

Here is an example of some wording that can be used if you decide that you are ready to discuss the situation with your supervisor:

"Bill, I wanted to let you know that I am going through a difficult divorce. Over the next few months, I hope that I can have some flexibility in case an emergency comes up that requires my attention."

"I am not asking for any special treatment. I will make up for any lost time by working extra hard after hours or on weekends if the job requires it. I will also do all that I can to schedule my appointments after or before work. However, this may be impossible at times, especially when dealing with court appearances, so I may have to take some time off to deal with this. I hope that you will understand."

"Also, I will let you know of any appointments as soon as I become aware of them. We can take a look together at our schedules and plan accordingly. If by any chance one of my appointments conflicts with a work meeting that is critical, I will do all in my power to have the appointment re-scheduled. Thank you very much for your understanding."

You are not begging for mercy or falling at his feet. Instead, you are informing him about what is going on in your life and setting the stage for some flexibility on his part down the road.

You can only have such a conversation with a supervisor who is reasonable and approachable. If you can have this conversation, you will accomplish two important things:

1. You will now have one less thing to worry about. Hopefully, your boss will be understanding and you can walk away knowing that in case of an emergency, you will be able to take care of the problem without the fear of losing your job.

2. You will demonstrate to your boss that you are indeed a dedicated and hard-working employee. You have shown that despite the situation, you are willing to put in the time to get the job done right. This shows maturity and reliability, and you have just turned a negative event into a positive one at work. How many of your co-workers would have the guts to say what you said?

Now let's talk about a more complicated case. There certainly are going to be cases where a boss behaves in a manner that is anything but reasonable. Some might use your situation against you, and your job may be at risk because of the pressures imposed by the divorce.

If you feel that you have an unreasonable supervisor who will use the divorce against you, ***do not jeopardize your work by having such a conversation.*** Instead, you will have to use different tactics so as not to interfere with your job.

The first thing that you need to do is schedule meetings with your lawyer during off-hours. Lawyers are accustomed to dealing with people like you and will often be available late in the evening or on weekends. Make sure that you take this fact into account when choosing a lawyer and inform him or her right away about the volatile situation that you face at work.

The next thing that you can do is utilize any co-workers that you are friendly with in the office to your advantage. Even though your boss may not be approachable, perhaps you have allies that would be happy to help you out and cover for you in case of an emergency. Perhaps you can help out a co-worker and swap favors with him another time.

If you feel that the situation at work is so volatile, plan ahead for the coming year by conserving your vacation days and sick days religiously. In your situation, it would not be a wise idea to take a vacation and blow a week or two weeks of vacation time. Save the days! By scheduling lawyer meetings during off hours and using vacation and sick days for court appearances, you may be able to get through the divorce without affecting your job.

The key is to understand your current position and devise a plan. Let me recap some of these ideas:

1. If at all possible, discuss the impending divorce with your boss and ask for flexibility in the future, while asserting your dedication to the job.

2. Schedule your appointments with your lawyer during off-hours, either after work or on weekends.

3. Utilize any allies that you have in the office to help you out if your boss is unapproachable.

4. Start conserving your vacation days, sick days and/or personal days right now, since you may need those days for court appearances during the divorce.

What You Say & Do Counts-Starting Today!

During the divorce proceedings you will find yourself in emotional situations that you have never encountered before. A divorce can bring out the worst of anyone. You will feel hurt, angry, cheated, and probably miserable.

Your feelings belong to you alone; they can remain in your heart or be shared with loved ones if you so choose. You can be as angry as you like and pummel a punching bag to your heart's content. However, your *actions* from this point forward will play a critical role in the divorce. It is time to take a close look at yourself and become mentally prepared for what lies ahead.

Ask yourself the following questions:

*   Are you easily upset?

*   Do you get angry and raise your voice?

*   Do you find that you do or say things that you later regret?

*   Do you lose control of your emotions under pressure?

*   Do you have a tendency to behave violently?

You may ask, "Whose business is it how I act?" In your current situation, the answer is very simple:
"How you act during the divorce proceedings can have a profound effect on the ultimate resolution!"

Think about some of the issues that will be addressed during the divorce. Both you and your wife will make claims. Anyone has the right to claim whatever his or her heart desires. The court, however, will not simply rely on statements and will look for factual proof. The judge will be looking for ways to determine who is trustworthy, sincere, and dependable. If children are involved in the case, the court must determine who is best fit to have custody.

Do your words or actions play a role in helping the court determine who you are and what you are capable of doing? Of course they do! Therefore, it is critical that you begin today to watch every word that you say and every action that you take when it comes to your wife, the court and everyone else in your life.

Imagine a husband who is vilified as cruel and abusive. Claims are made that he never spent any time with his children and refused to provide for them while his wife had no source of income or savings. Does such a claim in and of itself represent proof? Not really. However, picture the same husband in a court setting losing his temper and screaming that his wife is a liar! His own lawyer cannot control him and the judge must ask that he refrain from talking or he will be held in contempt of court.

Who will the judge be more inclined to believe? Will he believe the wife, who is sitting quietly, or the husband who appears to be out of control and irrational.

I am not suggesting that you should put on a happy face and always keep your mouth shut. There will be times when you will have to stand up for yourself and fight for the principles that you believe in. You need to be cautious about what you say and how you say it since everything that is done during the proceedings will be carefully scrutinized and can work either for you or against you in the final resolution.

Too many men fail to grasp this simple concept. How many times have men explicitly shown the court that they have quick tempers and that they can't control themselves? I have heard of husbands who have threatened their wives during the proceedings in front of witnesses. Others have written nasty letters, telling their wives what they are going to do to them and how much pain they will inflict upon them. During my first court experience, I watched a lawyer pull out a letter that a husband had written to his client, the wife. In the letter the husband stated that he would get the wife, and that he would send his people to her at any time to harm her in violent ways. The husband was viewed as a lunatic, and his chances of walking away with a resolution in his favor were damaged. Do you think that any of these men were better off for acting in such a way? Were their causes served?

Here is a small sample of some of the things that men have done during their divorce proceedings that have come back to haunt them. Think about each one and ask how this could have impacted their divorce.

1. Lost control in court and yelled at and threatened his wife

2. Got angry with the judge and shouted comments during the proceedings

3. Grabbed his wife and physically assaulted her

4. Demonstrated a tendency towards violence by arguing with or shoving court employees and security personnel

5. Made threats to his wife, members of her family, lawyers, court employees and even the judge

6. Wrote nasty and hostile letters to his wife, members of her family, lawyers, court employees and the judge

7. Continued to interrupt the judge

8. Cursed his wife and her lawyer in front of the judge

9. Used hand gestures to signify to his wife from across the room just what he thought of her

Don't be one of the men who destroy themselves by losing sight of their goals. You are smarter than that! You *must* act smarter from this point forward.

What you have done or said in the past cannot be changed now. If you regret having performed hurtful acts or saying harmful words, you will have to face the consequences of those actions and move forward. From this point on you **do** have control over yourself and your actions. You **can** think long and hard before you say or do something that will be hurtful to your cause. You **must** learn how to keep your emotions in check if you want to survive the divorce.

Let's take a look at one simple way for you to do this.

We have all heard or read about the advances in technology that have taken place over the past ten years in the area of surveillance. Everywhere you go, there is a chance you may be being watched by a hidden camera, and every word that you say could potentially be caught on tape. Your wife can even purchase a professional, high-quality telephone recorder at RadioShack for fifty dollars.

From this point forward, act and speak as if you are being watched and recorded at all times. Think about every move that you make and ask yourself if you would still act the same way if a tape of you were to be shown in the courtroom on the following day. When you have conversations with your wife, or anyone else for that matter regarding the divorce, ask yourself if you would say the same things if a recording of the conversation were to be played in court. Besides the fact that it is certainly possible that you are being taped, it is more important to recognize that all that you do could come back to haunt you. Instead, say things that can only help your cause. Speak as if the judge were listening to your words and convince him or her of your sincerity.

Being conscious of what you do and say is not a matter of strategy. If for some reason you strategize that you must say something seemingly derogatory to your wife, that decision is yours to make. At a minimum, think about what you are doing and saying and be certain you honestly feel that it is in your best interest.

Take the case of a husband whose wife is attempting to extort an exorbitant sum in monthly alimony payments. The husband has the sense that the wife is just trying to get as much as she can but is not willing to go the distance with the process and actually fight for this amount in a court of law. The husband could decide to tell the wife that he will not give in and is prepared to do whatever it takes to not pay what he believes to be an unreasonable amount, no matter what the legal costs would be. By doing this, he is hopeful that the wife will accept a lower amount by way of an agreement and avoid a trial altogether. I am not telling you to do this, but I can say that the husband is in control of his emotions and is acting in a way that he believes will help his case.

I am more concerned about what you do when you are *not* thinking. When you allow your emotions to get the better of you, you can potentially destroy yourself and your standing with the court.

Let's look at a father who is trying desperately to get custody of his children. He claims to be a great father but his wife states otherwise. Instead of speaking calmly to his wife or to the judge, he is argumentative and combative at every court appearance. He easily loses his temper and interrupts when others are speaking. Obviously, his chances of getting custody of his children are diminished.

So remember, now more than ever you cannot afford to make mistakes that you will later regret. From a practical standpoint, losing control of your emotions can negatively impact your position in the divorce proceedings. You can be perceived as an irrational and untrustworthy person, and your chances of walking away with a fair agreement are compromised. From a personal perspective, the pain that you cause another person in the heat of the moment could cause you an equal amount of pain. Take what others dish out with a grain of salt and learn to ignore someone if he or she is trying to get you agitated. This person would like nothing more that to upset you and make you lose control. Don't give him or her the satisfaction. Keep your dignity intact and learn to ignore combative people and walk away from volatile situations.

Act and speak as if you are being watched and recorded at all times and you will train yourself to be in total control of your emotions and avoid unnecessary pain and regret in the future.

If you feel you need some help, consider the following options:

- Seek short-term therapy to help you through the divorce

- Go to an anger management course

- Commit to getting in shape by eating right and exercising

- Ask your doctor about prescription medication to help you relax

- Seek out support groups in your area to boost your self-confidence

Despite all that has happened between you and your wife, you were both in love at some point and shared at least some good moments together. You also shared personal and confidential information with one another. During the heat of battle, some men have made the mistake of trying to hurt their wives by bringing up painful memories or by making light of their prior suffering. From speaking to a few men who have done this, the common theme that runs through their stories is that they regret what they have done so much and are pained themselves by the hurt that they caused their wife.

Once you do or say something, you can't take it back. Now is a time of confusion, pain and hurt; at this precise time in your life, you need to think long and hard about how much you are willing and able to hurt another person. In the heat of a dispute you can easily say anything, but after all the dust has settled, you will have to live with what you said for the rest of your life.

Take my word for it—it's not worth it. You may want to hurt the other person so badly, but at the end, you are probably hurting yourself more. One of the most difficult things for me to deal with to this day (and I have been divorced for 10 years as I write this) is the pain that I caused others during my divorce. I wish that I could take back some of the things that I said to my ex-wife and to members of her family. In the heat of the moment, my emotions sometimes got the better of me.

Stay in control of your emotions and think about how much you may regret saying or doing something. You are in the middle of a war, but it will end and you will return to a normal life again. How many scars would you like to have when the war is over?

CHAPTER 4

▼

TOPICS OF DIVORCE

During this transitional phase of your life, you and your wife will wrestle with issue after issue, trying desperately to come to an arrangement. Some of these issues will be simple and easily resolved; others, however, might turn out to be extremely complex and require the involvement of experts.

Now is the time to begin to familiarize yourself with some of the topics that typically arise in any divorce proceeding. The reasons for doing this are twofold:

1. You need to understand what topics specifically relate to you so that you can start to focus your attention on them.

2. Once you have an idea as to what issues you will encounter, you can begin to formulate your aspirations of how you would like each issue to ultimately be decided.

Every divorce case has some unique issues that must be addressed. In general, however, the topics described in this section represent standard ones that you will encounter and that you <u>must</u> begin to think about.

Your goal is not to become an expert on these topics. Instead, the issues are listed here to help you determine which relate specifically to you. As you go through the topics, you should view them from a "final agreement" perspective. In other words, one way or another, the resolution to these topics must be outlined in a final agreement that you reach or in a court judgment that is passed down. Start imagining how you would like to see them resolved. Identify those issues that are most important to you and those that are less important. Think about what topics you would be inclined to give in on and which topics you might be willing to go to great lengths to fight for.

Don't worry about formulating a strategy right know for the divorce and don't think that you need to know exactly how you will advance on each individual topic. Your goal right now is to identify those issues that relate to your case and consider how you would like to see them resolved.

I have grouped the topics into three broad categories:

1. **General**

2. **You and Your Wife**

3. **Children**

There are some *general* topics of divorce. These topics are high-level issues that you should think about when formulating your own idea of a final divorce agreement or verdict.

After that, I list some issues that *you and your wife* will undoubtedly encounter, whether or not there are any children involved in the divorce.

Finally, any divorce that involves a child or a number of **children** inherently possesses a different level of complexity than a divorce that does not. When a child is involved, the issues revolving around the child such as custody and visitation take center stage and the resolution of those issues drive the process.

My hope is that by reading about some of these topics, a light will go on in your head and you will realize that there are many important issues that you have not thought about before in the context of the divorce. What about that 401K from one of your earlier jobs? What about that life insurance policy you took out 2 years ago? Will your ex-wife be able to move to a different state or even country with your children after the divorce? Who gets the dog?

General Issues

Agreement vs. Trial

From the onset, it is crucial that you understand the difference between reaching an agreement with your wife and having the court reach a verdict via a trial.

If you are able to reach an agreement with your wife, the final costs of the divorce will be considerably lower than if the case goes to trial. There are usually many issues that both the husband and the wife can agree upon, and only a few controversial points that must be ironed out before an agreement can be reached.

Alternatively, some divorce cases go to trial. This means that a judge will decide who gets to keep what and also who must make payments and in what amounts. Going to trial will cost you a tremendous amount of time and money and the results are hard to predict in advance.

It would be impossible to make a blanket statement that you should never go to trial. Of course, it would be beneficial to you and your wife to jointly reach an agreement and potentially save tens of thousands of dollars. Going to trial will mean that all of your dirty laundry will be aired out in a public setting. Most people do not have the stomach to dish out this type of dirt or have it dished out against them. Reaching an agreement will save everyone time, money and emotional grief and anguish. However, there may be times when a trial is your only option. If your wife is making demands that you simply can't meet, a trial may be right for you. If you honestly believe in your heart that your wife is not fit to care for your children, you may decide that you will fight for the well-being of your children at all costs. You may be dealing with an irrational person who simply refuses to agree with you on any issue, and you may be forced by her to go to trial despite your best intentions.

There are risks and benefits to both sides. While an agreement is ideal, it is not always possible. Some might prefer the sense of control that an agreement provides over the uncertainty of going to trial and having a judge decide your fate. This could even mean that you agree to terms that are less favorable than what you had hoped for in order to avoid a trial altogether. Some may feel that they would like to reach an agreement, but simply cannot compromise their principles or the safety of their children.

Where do you fit on the spectrum of agreement versus trial? Can you visualize yourself reaching an agreement with your wife? Can you both look past the hurt and pain of the breakup and try to dissolve the marriage as amicably as possible? Or do you see a more complicated and destructive road up ahead? Hopefully, you will see the benefits of reaching an agreement with your wife through your respective attorneys. If she too wants to work out the details of the divorce in a civil and respectable way, you will finalize your divorce quickly and efficiently. If your wife is unwilling to compromise, it might take some time for her to come to her senses or you may ultimately be forced to go to trial.

Divorce Mediation

Since I have discussed the differences between reaching an agreement and going to trial, it behooves me to say a word about the concept of divorce mediation. A divorce mediator is an attorney that works with both you and your wife together to settle the divorce. The mediator will review the issues with you, give an opinion as to how the court would likely rule and help draft a final divorce agreement that both parties and the judge will sign.

The nature of many divorces precludes the concept of a divorce mediator from even being discussed. If the divorce is contested, or if there are wide gaps between the expectations of the two parties, a mediator would not be practical. If, however, both you and your wife are reasonable, and there is a general agreement to get divorced as expediently and as cheaply as possible, a mediator may be your best option.

To my own surprise, I see more and more mediators popping up all the time. I can speak from experience that the mediation approach did not work very well for me. I sat through one session and realized that our expectations were so far apart that we needed separate lawyers to protect our interests, and I paid $1,500.00.

A friend of mine named Harold also sought mediation. The mediator asked his wife what she would like to get out of the divorce. The wife said that she would like to take the chandelier in the kitchen and break it over Harold's head. The mediator then suggested that perhaps Harold and his wife should seek separate representation.

The fact that people are using mediators suggests that there are more people getting divorced who have only been married for a short period of time. There are less joint assets involved in the divorce and no children. That type of scenario is ripe for a mediator.

Using a mediator will translate into low costs, a relatively quick divorce and a potentially painless process. The trouble is that it simply is not practical for many divorce cases today.

Martin and Carole were childless. They had been married for three years. He was an accountant; she was a dentist. They had no significant assets other than some cash and investments. They had no hard feelings towards one another; they had simply grown apart. They sought an amicable divorce and went to a mediator. The mediator helped them distribute the assets, agree upon who will keep the apartment and who would move out, and write up the settlement agreement.

The divorce took only a few months. It cost a few thousand dollars and not tens of thousands of dollars like other divorce cases.

Can a mediator work for you? Can you and your wife sit down together with an objective third party and work out all of the issues that you face? If so, a divorce mediator may be a good place to start the process.

If you do decide to use a divorce mediator, I recommend that you still research the issues on your own and seek legal advice from an outside lawyer that can guide you through the process. While the mediator may be looking to reach a deal as quickly as possible, an independent attorney can review the agreement and give you his or her expert opinion on whether or not the agreement is reasonable. If the agreement is so grossly skewed in favor of your wife, you can decide to abandon the process and seek independent counsel. If the agreement is not great, but it falls within a reasonable range, you may decide to move forward in order to avoid more costly legal fees and unnecessary pain in the future.

Uncontested vs. Contested

Directly related to the issue of reaching agreement or going to trial are the terms 'uncontested' and 'contested.' An uncontested divorce is one where both parties agree to the divorce; a contested divorce is where one side argues against the divorce or takes the case to court for a judge to decide the final outcome.

Many divorces begin as contested since only one party initiates the divorce. Ultimately, most of these cases wind up as uncontested anyway since the other party comes to his or her senses and deals with the reality of the situation. There may be legal and strategic reasons to contest a divorce, but it is important to note that a contested divorce will go to trial, and a judge will decide if the divorce will be granted. This same judge will determine the resolutions to all of the issues that are discussed below and tell you exactly what you must do for the next ten or twenty years of your life.

Do you believe that your own divorce will be uncontested or contested? Have you and your wife discussed the possibility of divorce beforehand, or have you totally shocked your wife or been shocked yourself upon receiving divorce papers? Did she see it coming? Did you see it coming?

Grounds for Divorce

The laws related to the grounds for divorce differ from state to state. In general, there are some states where a couple can get a divorce based on irreconcilable differences; in other states, actual grounds for the divorce are required.

These grounds include adultery, abandonment, constructive abandonment (which is the refusal by one spouse to have sexual relations with the other) and cruel treatment of one spouse by the other.

I'll be perfectly honest here: these laws are archaic and should be changed. They are responsible for many ugly divorces. Rather than allowing a couple to get divorced with dignity, these laws force the parties to become involved in a battle that is unnecessary. Sure you may want a divorce, but does that mean that you will allow your wife to claim that you committed adultery or treated her in a cruel manner. Why should you have to agree to such a thing? If you live in a state that requires grounds for the divorce, you must familiarize yourself with the concept since the laws will not be changed any time soon.

The grounds for divorce are not placed on your record as a criminal offense, so no matter what the grounds are, it really does not matter. If you can ignore the grounds and focus on the final result, you will be better off.

Having said that, people are not so willing to allow false statements to be made about them, so you would be wise to focus your attention on "constructive abandonment" as so many couples have done in the past. Most of us can agree to the fact that you have not had relations with your wife for a year. This does not necessarily reflect negatively on you. You may even have been separated or involved in the divorce proceedings for that amount of time. It sure beats adultery and cruel and unusual treatment! The judge won't pay a visit to your bedroom and investigate. On the contrary. The judge wants to give the divorce as much as you want to get it, but he or she needs to follow the law and must have a reason to grant the divorce. Make it easy on the judge and on yourselves by using grounds for the divorce that you and your wife can both live with and that no one can contradict.

Be Specific

Hopefully, you will be able to work out an agreement with your wife that you can both live with. As you work toward that end, remember the importance of being clear and specific in the agreement on every issue. Now is the time that the agreement will be drafted and finalized, and now is the time to make sure that there is nothing ambiguous about it.

Of course your lawyer will look over the agreement and make sure that the standard clauses are included. But you too must be absolutely certain that there will be no questions down the road. It will be much harder to clarify a section of the agreement in your favor once the agreement is signed and sealed. It would be a tremendous financial and emotional burden for you to take the agreement back to court and contest the ambiguity of a clause. Make sure that as the agreement is being drafted all statements are clear and concise and that there will be no argument later on as to what is actually meant by a clause.

On the other hand, you will not be able to predict everything that will occur over the next ten or twenty years. There must be some degree of flexibility in the agreement that allows for mutual changes to be made. I recommend that the agreement should specifically state that both parties could agree to a different term if they so choose.

For example, suppose that an agreement is drafted that specifies the schools that the children can attend. Four schools are listed and the agreement states that the mother may send the child to only one of these four schools. The agreement should also state that both parties could agree to send the children to a different school if they so desire. Alternatively, the agreement could state that if the parties cannot reach an agreement as to how to resolve an issue, they agree to adhere to the ruling of a specified arbitrator.

You cannot predict the future, but you can allow for a degree of flexibility in the agreement while detailing exactly how a resolution will be reached. While a resolution to an issue may not always be spelled out in the agreement, there should be no ambiguity as to the "method" that will be used to reach agreement on every topic that you could possibly face.

Choose Inclusion over Exclusion

In addition to making the agreement clear, concise, and free of ambiguity, you may have some questions about what to include and what to omit. Should you include items that seem silly, like who will get the rug in the living room or the extra linens? Who will get the picture hanging in the bathroom?

As a general rule, if something is important to you, make sure that you include it in the agreement. Divorce agreements in the past have included anything and everything, from goldfish to pillowcases to garbage cans. If an item is important to you, don't hope that your wife will not care about it. Don't assume that something automatically belongs to you. Put it in the agreement! Specify as much as possible and don't be afraid to include everything that is important to you.

Now is your only chance. Once the agreement is signed, it will be very difficult to make changes. Think long and hard about the issues that you care about and make sure that they are included in any agreement that you reach or in any trial verdict that is handed down. It's basically now or never, so don't waste the opportunity.

You and Your Wife

Separate Residence—Marital Home

You and your wife have shared a home or an apartment during the marriage. As part of the divorce settlement, a decision must be made as to who will occupy the residence going forward or how the residence will be divided.

If you and your wife lived in a home that was owned by you, either you will continue to live in the home, or your wife will live in the home from this point forward. The agreement must be clear as to who will assume any outstanding mortgage on the home and any other issues related to upkeep. The home might be sold on the open market with the proceeds going to both parties. Here too, the agreement must be clear as to exactly how it will be sold, how the proceeds will be divided and who will be responsible for organizing the sale and the distribution of the cash.

If you lived in an apartment, the agreement must spell out what will happen to the apartment after the divorce. It should state who will be allowed to live in the apartment, who will be responsible for any liabilities related to the lease on the apartment, who will be responsible for paying rent, and what name will appear on the lease agreement. A divorce agreement would typically state that within a certain number of days from the signing of the agreement the person that will continue to live in the apartment must remove the name of the other person from the lease contract.

Division of Property

The agreement should spell out exactly what each party will get when the divorce is concluded. An important term for you to become familiar with is "commingled." In many jurisdictions, the concept of commingling an asset will determine which party has rights to the asset.

Commingling refers to the act of mixing or joining an asset into the pot of joint marital assets. For example, suppose that you had a bank account before the marriage. During the marriage, you never touched the bank account and did not make any deposits to the account or withdrawals from the account. This asset would typically be considered a separate asset belonging to the husband and not a "joint" asset of the marriage. On the other hand, if the husband made deposits to the account during the marriage and wrote checks for joint expenses, the account might now be deemed to be a commingled asset and jointly owned by both parties.

Any income that was earned during the marriage is generally considered to be a joint marital asset, and in addition, any assets that were brought into the marriage but commingled into joint accounts are also considered to be joint marital assets that must be distributed to both parties. Thinking back to the section on "Getting Organized," it is clear why you may need to prove that some assets are actually owned by you alone and should not be considered as part of the joint marital assets.

The agreement should outline all of the assets that each person will keep. If there is an asset that is important to you, you must make sure that it is included in the agreement. Here are just a few items that may be applicable to your own divorce settlement:

- Homes and other properties
- Boats
- Cars
- Clothing
- Jewelry
- Books
- Linens
- Furniture
- Electronics
- Rugs
- China & Flatware
- Bank accounts, both checking and savings
- Brokerage accounts
- Custodial accounts of the children
- Retirement & Pension funds
- 401K plan balances
- Musical Instruments
- Pets
- Exercise Equipment

- Paintings and portraits

- Pictures

Think about everything that you own and make sure that they are somehow included in the agreement. If you care about an item, add it into the agreement now.

In addition to the types of assets listed above, any professional license that was earned during the marriage might be considered to be joint marital property. (Seems a little unfair, but it is the law). The agreement must spell out exactly what each party is entitled to with regards to the license, or at a minimum state that the parties waive their rights to such licenses in the future. The important factors that a court might look at with regards to licenses are:

- Who paid for the license?

- How much of the license was earned before the marriage?

- What is the value of the license, calculated as the present value of the future earnings of the license? (An actuary would typically calculate such a figure).

In addition to stating the assets that each party will retain, the agreement should lay out the method of taking possession of such assets.

For example, an agreement could state that within a certain number of days from the signing of the agreement, the husband will have the right to pick up items A, B & C from the marital residence provided that he give the wife notice. The agreement may state that certain accounts will remain under the ownership of the current name listed on the account, or that an account must be transferred to the wife or to the husband within a specified number of days.

Knowing what you are entitled to is important. Having a signed agreement that outlines how you should take possession of the asset with the court's approval is also crucial.

Maintenance/Alimony

These are dreaded words that no man likes to hear. The terms "maintenance" and "alimony" mean the same thing, so don't get confused when you hear them used. Maintenance is generally used in a legal setting. It refers to payments made by one spouse to the other after the divorce. While there are cases of alimony payments from the wife to the husband, more cases result in alimony payments being made from the husband to the wife, although this trend is shifting as more and more women move up the corporate ladder and enter high-salaried positions. If you are a husband that will receive alimony payments, I tip my hat to you and salute you, for you are a fortunate man.

For the rest of us, here are a few things that you need to know. Any divorce agreement should specify whether or not alimony payments will be made. The amount should be clearly stated, and more importantly, the amount of time that the payments will continue should be outlined. For example, an agreement could state that "starting on January 1, 2003 and for a period of three years ending on January 1, 2006 …" The agreement should also state the manner in which the payment should be made, i.e. by check or money order.

You also need to be clear as to what events would cause the payments to cease. For example, alimony will typically end if the wife remarries or if either the wife or husband dies. Think about the following factors that play a role in determining the amount and duration of alimony payments and see if you are a candidate.

- How long were you married? The longer the marriage, the better the chances are that you will pay alimony.

- Did your wife work during the marriage? If your wife stayed home and watched the kids, your chances of paying alimony increase. If your wife worked and is able to support herself, alimony might not be appropriate.

- Does your wife have the skills to support herself? If your wife has no skills, the court might hold you responsible for maintaining her accustomed lifestyle until she is able to acquire some type of work skill.

- What type of lifestyle did you lead? If you showered your wife with fine clothes and expensive jewelry, there is a good chance that you will be required to make alimony payments so that she can maintain her standard of living.

Remember, the idea of 'lifestyle' will play a major role in determining the alimony issue since it is the desire of the court that the husband and wife maintain their current lifestyles after the divorce. The lifestyle argument outweighs all of the other factors listed above. If a wife lived a luxurious life during the marriage but was only married for six months, it will be hard to argue that she has grown accustomed to such a lavish lifestyle in so short a time span. If a wife had a lavish lifestyle but also worked during the marriage, the court would be less inclined to allow for alimony payments since the wife is accustomed to working and has the means to support herself. If the wife has the skills necessary to work but did not utilize those skills during the marriage, the court may still provide for alimony payments but possibly for a lesser amount of time so that the wife can ease her way back into the workplace.

Taking all of these factors into account, where do <u>you</u> stand? Look back at the section titled "Getting Organized" and start gathering the data that that you will need to boost your case.

One final note on alimony. Alimony is taxable to the wife who receives it and tax deductible to the husband who pays it. That means that you can reap huge benefits by structuring your payments as alimony as opposed to something else. Child support payments and any lump-sum payments to the wife in lieu of joint assets are not tax deductible.

If it is clear that you will need to make payments to your wife for whatever reason, it is best to structure such payments as alimony. This is sometimes made possible by the fact that your wife may expect to report very little income in the upcoming years while you plan to report substantial income. Since the wife's income is so low, she may not care whether or not the payments are taxable since she will not pay taxes on them anyway and is just happy to get the money. You, on the other hand, would be much better off with the tax write-off and could potentially save thousands of dollars.

In short, if you are already making payments, try as hard as you can to have them classified as alimony. Even if you just hate the idea of paying alimony and it tears you up inside to see that word in your divorce agreement, your tax refund at the end of the year will bring a smile to your face, and you will forget about the divorce when you cash the check.

Responsibility for Debts

If you or your wife have outstanding loans or debts, the agreement should outline who is liable for such loans and who is not. Just because your wife's name is on her loans, don't assume that she will take responsibility for them. The agreement should clearly state that you are not liable for such loans and that your wife is responsible for paying them. The same would apply to your own loans.

Oftentimes, such debts are forgotten, and only after an agreement is reached do they rise to the surface. Think about the following items and ask yourself if any apply to your case.

- Student loans taken out by you

- Student loans taken out by your wife

- Mortgages

- Financing for a car

- Credit card balances

- Any other loans that you or your wife might have taken

The issue of outstanding debt can become complex when both you and your wife took out a loan but utilized only one name on the loan. In this case, it may be necessary to prove that the loan proceeds were used by both parties and that the loan should now be assumed jointly by you and your wife. Gathering the required documentation would be critical to making such a claim.

Life Insurance Policy

If you are going to pay either alimony or child support, you could also be required to maintain a life insurance policy for the amount of future payments that you must make. Basically, your payments are viewed as an outstanding debt by you and the court could say that your wife and children must be cared for in the event you die.

Make sure that the agreement states the amount of the policy, the beneficiary of the policy, the amount of time that you must maintain the policy, and most importantly, the trustee of the policy on behalf of a minor. If the life insurance policy were to name a child as the beneficiary, you may not want it to fall into the hands of your wife. Agree upon a trustee that you both know will distribute the money to your child in a fair and equitable manner. Sometimes, Rabbis or Priests are chosen to act as trustees if they agree to do so since both parties trust them and believe that they are impartial.

You can get a term life insurance policy at a very affordable price, and if your wife ever benefits from it, you won't care too much because you'll already be dead.

Sharing of Financial Documentation

At times, calculations for payments are made based upon the relative incomes of the husband and wife. For example, child support, which is described further below under the section on *Children*, will typically be calculated as a percentage of gross income. In addition, other payments such as childcare expenses and tuition might be calculated on a pro-rata basis to the respective incomes of both the husband and the wife.

The theory is based upon an 'ability to pay' approach where the parent with the greatest ability to pay the expense bears the heaviest burden.

The agreement must provide the means for objectively calculating these payments, and the calculations can only be achieved through the sharing of financial information. More specifically, you and your wife will probably have to exchange your tax returns for a number of years or for as long as such payments are made. The agreement should specify exactly when you are required to share the tax returns and also how the relevant calculations should be made.

Religious Divorce

For Jewish couples that are seeking a divorce, the issue of a religious divorce or the "get" oftentimes plays a major role in the proceedings. We have all heard the stories about husbands who refused to give the "get" to their wives, and as such, these women are precluded from getting re-married. The issue can become ugly.

There are a few important points to note with regards to the "get" that you should think about. Any divorce agreement should also have a section on the religious divorce and the procedure that must be followed with regards to the "get." Your wife will certainly want a guarantee that the "get" will be given without any problems. You, on the other hand, also want the agreement to mention the "get," but for a very different reason.

The Jewish marriage contract usually includes a monetary payment that the husband must make to the wife in case of a divorce. Men do not typically think clearly about divorce issues when they are in love and getting married, and do not pay much attention or even know about the amount that is specified in the marriage license, known as the Ketubah. I have heard of cases where amounts of eighteen thousand dollars or even one hundred thousand dollars were written into the Ketubah. Your job is to make sure that all of the monetary issues are included in the body of the divorce agreement and that the payment outlined in the Ketubah is waived and declared null and void.

Imagine how stressful it would be to finalize an agreement and have it accepted by the court, only to be told later on that you must pay an additional amount!

While your wife wants a guarantee on receiving the "get," you should get a guarantee that any amount in the Ketubah will not be enforced. These desires can be used to offset one another and a typical agreement might state that within a certain number of days from the signing of the divorce agreement, the husband agrees to give the "get," the wife agrees to accept it, and all monetary payments noted in the Ketubah are waived.

Children

Custody

The crucial question with regards to a child is who will get custody. Factors weighed when deciding the question of custody include the ability of the father or mother to support the child financially, the amount of hours that each parent works, the emotional stability of each parent, the prior relationship of each parent with the child, the age of the child and possibly the child's own wishes if the child is old enough and mature enough to voice them.

Many think that the issue of custody is black or white; either

a.   Your wife will get custody and the child will live with her

b.   You will get custody and the child will live with you or

c.   Both you and your wife will have 'split custody' of the child and the child will stay with your wife half the time and with you half the time.

However, the choices above are solely focused on the "physical" custody of the child. The concept of "legal" custody is critical to any decision that you will make with regards to your child. You should think of legal custody as the acknowledgement that no matter where the child actually lives, both you and the mother are equal parents in the eyes of the law.

From a practical standpoint, this means that both parents will keep one another informed of the whereabouts of the child. Both the father and the mother must jointly make major medical decisions for the child. They will both decide what schools and camps the child attends. They will both have access to any information from the child's doctor, teacher, school or camp.

Thus, you should look at custody through two different lenses, and the agreement should ultimately address both the physical custody of the child and the legal custody.

The distinction between physical custody and legal custody helps many couples reach an agreement on the issue without resorting to a trial. Let's take a look at a father and mother who are both relatively good parents and who both love their child. Many men would agree to the fact that a split physical custody arrangement is probably not in the best interest of the child. A child needs consistency and a place to call home, and the idea of making a young kid change places every three and a half days does not lead to stability. Here's where legal custody comes into play. Many divorce agreements are structured in such a way that one parent gets physical custody of the child, the other parent gets visitation rights, and both parents have legal custody of the child.

If your situation is more complicated, and you decide to fight for physical custody of your child, there's one thing that you should know as a man. While some men do get custody of their children, you are facing an uphill battle. Courts are not quick to take a child away from the mother, and you will have to prove that it is in the best interest of the child to stay with you as opposed to the mom. It is not impossible for you to get custody and some men actually do succeed, but the burden is all on you. You will have to prove that you are fit to be the custodian of the child and that the mother is not, and that is not an easy task.

Where do you stand on the issue? Do you think that you can work out an arrangement of joint legal custody? Is custody even important to you, or are you happy with reasonable visitation rights? Do you envision a long custody battle ahead? Are you just trying to aggravate your wife? What do you really want? What do think is in the best interest of the child?

Visitation

The next issue is directly linked to custody. Barring a split custody arrangement where the child spends half of the time with each parent, one parent will probably have physical custody of the child while the other parent will have visitation rights. The age of the child, and as a consequence, the child's own social life, plays a role in the visitation schedule. The divorce agreement should spell out how visitation will work and exactly when you will see your child and on what terms.

This is sometimes difficult for men to swallow. I have heard men say, "Someone will dictate when I will see my own kids? I'll see them when I want to see them." I understand how you feel, but you need to focus here on the divorce agreement and the law. I hope that despite the plan that is laid out in the agreement, you and your wife will be flexible when it comes to visitation and work out what is best as different situations arise. Now, however, is the time to make sure that your rights are clearly defined and that you will have the option of spending a considerable amount of time with your child. You need to protect yourself and make sure that there will be no questions down the road as to how and when your visitation will take effect.

Here are a few issues that should be outlined in the agreement on visitation:

- Who will pick up and return the child?

- Where will the child generally be picked up?

- What will the procedure be if the child is sick?
- On what days will visitation occur?
- From what time until what time does the visitation last?
- On what religious or secular holidays will the father (or mother) have visitation rights?

The agreement should mention all religious holidays that will be divided between the parents. Historically, some couples have chosen to spend the same holidays with the child every year. For example, the child spends Passover or Easter with the father and Succoth or Christmas with the mother every year. Others have chosen to alternate holidays from year to year. For example, the child spends Easter with the father on even numbered years and with the mother on odd numbered years.

In addition to the religious holidays that specifically pertain to you, there are secular holidays and personal days that should be mentioned. These include:

- New Year's Day
- President's Day
- Labor Day
- Columbus Day
- Martin Luther King Day
- Memorial Day
- July 4th
- Veteran's Day
- Thanksgiving Day
- Mother's Day & Father's Day
- The child's birthday
- The mother's birthday
- The father's birthday

The agreement should be clear about which days supersede the others in cases of conflicting visitation rights. For example, if a religious holiday that the child would spend with the mother falls out on a secular holiday that the child spends with the father, the agreement should state which type of holiday has precedence.

Summer Visitation

Summer visitation should be viewed as separate and distinct from the normal visitation schedule of the school year. In the summertime, there is much more flexibility, and whether or not the child stays home, goes to camp or travels, the summer presents a great opportunity to spend time with your child.

The age of the child will play a key role. The agreement might specify different summer schedules for the different ages of the child. In general, the parent that has visitation rights during the school year and not primary physical custody should expect to have extended visitation in the summertime. Some agreements specify that half the summer be spent with the mother while half the summer be spent with the father. Other agreements actually allow for the child to spend the entire summer with the non-custodial father. The agreement should specify the dates of the visitation, as well as whether or not the custodial parent will have his or her own visitation rights during this extended period of time.

The point for you to remember is that if you receive visitation rights during the school year, you should make sure to separate the summer from the rest of the year and determine a stand-alone visitation schedule. This schedule should allow for more visitation or 'vacation' time for the non-custodial parent. For many men, the summer is the greatest opportunity for them to solidify a lasting relationship with their child. I take my vacation from work in the summer and spend several weeks with my daughter. It is the greatest time of the year, and I am able to connect with her in ways that I am unable to during the school year. There is something special about spending extended time with someone, as opposed to just one night here or there.

Child Support

The term child support relates to the payments made by the non-custodial parent to the custodial parent to provide for the child's basic necessities. The money should go toward items such as food, shelter, clothing, etc.

If it bothers you to make your child support payments, just remember that the money is going to your own kid and that getting divorced from your wife does not mean that you have lost your child. Your children still need you, both emotionally and financially, especially during this difficult time in their lives. Hopefully, you can focus on the child and not get caught up with the fact that you are handing over a check to the mother.

In general, the payments are calculated as a percentage of the gross combined income of both parents, and each parent's contribution to that combined income. The financial records required for such calculations include your tax returns and W-2 forms. Remember, calculations are based on gross income and not the net income. This seems unfair since in today's world, your gross income is a very poor indicator of how much money you actually make, considering the taxes and other deductions that come out of your paycheck. Unfortunately, that's the law.

The calculations will be based upon your income, and as such, it is important that a proper assessment be made. If you have just received a pay raise, the court would say that it is appropriate to calculate the child support payments based upon the new salary, since the salary will be the same going forward. If, however, you work for yourself or on a commission basis, the fact that you had a magnificent year should not mean that you should have to pay exceedingly high child support payments forever. If this year's income exceeded the norm, your job will be to prove this and justify a calculation based upon an average income over the past few years. On the other hand, if your income was exceptionally low this year in relation to previous years, the mother will try to prove that an average income would be more appropriate.

In any event, now is the time to see to it that the correct calculation is made. It is always possible to request a 'change in circumstances' from the court later on to adjust the child support payments when unforeseen events occur, but that will cost you in terms of time and money. Don't wait until the agreement is signed to point out that the child support calculation is incorrect; prove your case now.

The final agreement should outline the following:

- The amount of child support payments to be made

- The calculation utilized in reaching the amount

- The regularity of the payments, i.e. once a week in advance or once a month in advance

- The method of payment, i.e. income deduction, check, cash or money order

- The steps that the recipient of the child support payments should take if the payments are in arrears for a specified period of time.

One final note on child support. The courts have really cracked down on 'deadbeat' dads. If you do not pay your child support payments, the law can come down on you in a variety of ways, including taking the money directly from your paycheck and publicizing your name through the local media. So not paying your child support payments could turn out to hurt you in more ways than you can imagine.

Other Expenses Outside of Child Support

If you thought that your financial responsibilities to your child ended with child support, you are in for a surprise. There are a number of other expenses that fall outside of the realm of child support that you may be responsible for, including childcare costs, education expenses, and medical coverage.

While there is no defined law as to how much each parent may be required to contribute to each of these, it is clear that both parents are jointly responsible for them, and as such, the agreement should outline how these expenses will be covered. In contrast to the child support calculation that relied on a strict formula, these expenses are viewed more on an 'ability to pay' basis and the courts look at the overall picture when determining how much each parent must contribute. If a father was already paying high child support payments and alimony, it would be difficult for him to cover additional costs as well. Your job will be to show that you will be left with very little for yourself to live on once the child support payments and possibly alimony payments are taken into account. Your wife will argue that the opposite is true.

Child Care Expenses: If your child is very young and requires a childcare provider so that your wife can either work or go to school, you could be responsible for paying a portion of this expense. The arrangement might be that you pay half of the expense, or alternatively you might pay a percentage of the expense based upon each parent's respective incomes. The expenses should be fully supported by documentation.

Education Costs: If your child attends a private school, your child support payments are not counted toward the tuition. These "education" costs can include tuition and registration fees as well as transportation to and from the school. In addition, summer camp expenses are also shared by both parents. Some arrangements call for these expenses to be shared equally by both parents. Others call for the expenses to be divided based upon the incomes of the parents on a pro-rata basis. Still others stipulate that one parent will bear the entire cost, based upon that parent's overwhelming ability to pay relative to the other parent.

Medical Insurance: Someone must provide medical coverage for the child, and the agreement should spell out exactly how the medical coverage issue will be decided. Like educational expenses, these costs can be allocated to the parents in multiple ways.

When calculating your own ability to support yourself once the divorce is finalized, be sure to take into account *all* of the expenses that you are responsible for. If you calculate that your payments will cause you to actually lose money each month, something is terribly wrong. Your argument should be that taking into account your already substantial financial requirements, there simply is not enough left in the pot for contributions to these types of expenses.

One technique that might help you in reaching an agreement on these issues is the idea of a "cap." A cap or "ceiling" can be used to put a maximum dollar amount on a number of combined expenses. For example, some expenses over-lap; it would not make sense for a child to be given full-time childcare when he or she also attends school. There may be some school and some childcare, but each one could not possibly be full-time. The agreement should include a cap on the joint education and childcare expenses that you are responsible for in a given month, thereby limiting your amount of exposure to such payments.

Tax Exemptions and Credits

Back to taxes. When finalizing the divorce, you may not want to think about the next most tortuous thing in the world, but you must. Only one of the parents can claim the child as a dependent and take advantage of any child credits. The agreement should state who will be able to claim the child and also state in which years each parent can do so.

Typically, the parents alternate years and take turns claiming the child as a dependent. Some parents calculate their tax returns under different scenarios, both with the child as a dependent and without, in order to identify the parent whose tax return would reap the greatest benefit by claiming the child. The gains could then be split between the parents. The agreement should be specific enough to identify a plan of action, but also flexible enough to allow the parents to do their own math, should they choose to work together. If the relationship between you and your wife is such that you are able to perform such a calculation and share the monetary benefits, go ahead. In many cases, it is just not worth the hassle and aggravation of calculating these amounts jointly, so you will be better off alternating years.

Limitations on Where the Child Can Live

If the mother has primary physical custody of the child, you may be worried that she could move to anywhere in the world. Could she move to another state or even country?

Many agreements include a clause that limits the ability of the mother to remove the child from the current location beyond an established limit. Typically, a limit based on miles is imposed, such as a clause that states that the mother cannot move the child from the current residence beyond a forty-five or sixty mile radius without the consent of the father.

The parents could jointly agree that the child can be moved to a more distant location. In the event that the father does not agree, the mother would have to petition the court and she will then be forced to prove that it is in the best interest of the child to make such a move. It is imperative that you see this clause in your own agreement. While the wife may feel a bit restricted, you still need to protect yourself and make sure that the law will be on your side should she decide to move and take the child with her.

Emancipation of the Child

Time moves faster than we tend to imagine, and you will want to know when all the child related payments will cease and when the child is considered to be an adult. Emancipation events generally include the following:

- Reaching the age of 21
- Marriage of the child
- Death of the child
- Full-time employment of the child

CHAPTER 5

▼

FOCUS ON TRUE
INTERESTS

At the Stern School of Business where I studied for my MBA in Finance, a number of courses that focused exclusively on negotiations were offered. Week after week we practiced the art of negotiation through simulated cases. One week I was an IBM executive trying to open a plant in Mexico. The next week I was working for the Disney Corporation negotiating a deal to open an amusement park in France. And in the classic negotiation situation, I was the purchaser of a home negotiating the price with the seller.

While taking these courses, I could not help but feel despair over my own divorce and others that I had witnessed. I wish that I could have acquired these skills prior to the divorce settlement. How much time and energy would I have saved? How much money in legal fees would have gone to better use? How many men find themselves in the midst of the most complex and important negotiation of their lives with absolutely no idea what to do and no prior experience to guide them through the process?

What was it that made me feel this way? What eye-opening secrets did I acquire in these negotiation classes that made me realize that I had missed the whole point in all of my earlier negotiations in life? Most importantly, how can this knowledge be shared with you right now to help you along in your own negotiations?

The answer is simple. The single most important concept that you must understand and that permeates every negotiation is the distinction between a firm position adopted by any party and their underlying interests.

The negotiation literature on this topic is extensive. Let me sum up the approach as follows: A firm position is a stated posture on an issue that appears to be beyond the scope of negotiation. For example, the seller of the house might say, "I will not accept anything less than $500,000 for the house." The buyer might say, "I will not pay anything more than $400,000 for this house." These are the positions that the negotiation players have adopted. The parties involved have not explained the rationale behind the position nor expressed their true desires with regards to the house. In short, the underlying *interests* of the parties have not been addressed.

The idea of interests focuses on the underlying wishes of both parties for an ultimate resolution. The interests give meaning to the positions taken and the underlying rationale behind them.

Let's look at the seller for a moment. The seller's neighbor may have recently sold his home for $500,000 and as such, the seller wants to sell his home for no less. The interest of this seller is to sell his own home for a price that is no less than the amount paid for the most recently sold house on the block. He may also wish to sell the house quickly so that he can move to his dream home in Florida. His position shares none of these thoughts.

Now let's look at the buyer. The buyer may only have $100,000 to spend and he feels that he is only capable of securing a mortgage for an additional $300,000. He is only willing to pay $400,000 for the house or for any house for that matter. His interest lies in the fact that he <u>cannot</u> spend more on a house. His price is not a reflection on the home that he is looking at. It is a reflection of his own situation and his financial ability to purchase the home.

Why should you care about interests?

Why is it anyone's business that the buyer wants to pay only $400,000? Why should you care about the reasons why the seller wants $500,000?

You must care about interests because without an understanding of the interests you will never be able to break out of negotiation impasses.

In the example above, the seller wants $500,000 and the buyer wants to pay only $400,000. End of story. Both the buyer and the seller can each walk away—

right? What else is there to talk about! A position is a position and neither party will budge.

What if, however, the parties begin to focus on interests? Now there may be room to negotiate, and most importantly, solutions could be proposed that meet the needs of each party.

Let's go back to the seller. Perhaps by looking at the sales price of the neighbor's house and his own in terms of price per square foot, it may actually turn out that he is receiving more per square foot than the neighbor received. Perhaps the comparison between his own home and that of his neighbor was not appropriate to begin with since the neighbor had a swimming pool and a separate driveway, while our seller has no swimming pool and only a shared driveway. Imagine that the current buyer was able to pay cash for the house and transact the deal faster than any other potential buyer by approximately four months. Understanding these facts could help the seller re-examine his initial position and possibly reach a deal that he can be happy with even if he does not receive exactly $500,000.

Now let's look at the buyer. Imagine that the house is truly worth $500,000 and that the market value appraisals confirm this. The buyer might feel that he has no choice but to look elsewhere. What if, however, the buyer and seller discuss the matter further and it turns out that the seller can recommend a mortgage broker who is known for his ability to secure mortgages despite lower than usual down payments. Perhaps this broker will be able to find a way for the buyer to finance the purchase of the house, even at a price of $500,000. Would the buyer be interested then? If the buyer truly loves the home and is able to acquire financing, could his initial position be re-examined at this point?

By looking at interests and not only positions, the buyer and seller increase their chances of reaching an agreement that satisfies both parties. A negotiation that focuses solely on positions is doomed from the start. Only when underlying interests emerge is there a chance for settlement.

I can think of no better application of this concept than in a divorce setting. The mother says, "I want custody." The father says, "I want custody." The wife says, "You have to pay me alimony for twenty years." The husband says, "May my body rot in hell before I pay you one cent." How could any settlement be reached?

Time and time again, couples adopt strong positions at the beginning of the negotiation and continue to hold on to those positions at all costs. Some of these cases end up going before the judge in a lengthy and costly trial. What happens to the cases that don't go to trial? Can it be that these couples are expert negotiators who know how to focus on interests?

I would suggest that the answer is no. Ultimately, these couples reach an agreement that they sign only after months and months of grueling negotiations. Both parties continue to hold on to their positions until the very end. In the final analysis, however, they begin to recognize that their interests are more important than their positions, and they find a way to reach a compromise, thereby avoiding a trial. Here too, so much time and energy goes to waste defending statements that were made and holding fast to initial positions taken.

True, this concept will not *always* work. There will be cases that go to trial due to the complexity of the case and the wide gaps that may exist between the desires of the two negotiating parties. If the parties adhere to their positions and do not delve deeper into the underlying interests, there is rarely even a chance of reaching a settlement. By focusing on interests, you can give yourself that fighting chance and set the stage for the possibility of a joint agreement. At least you will have a chance! Why not give that to yourself before throwing in the towel and allowing someone else to decide your fate.

I am not giving you any divorce *strategies* either. I am not telling you to call up your wife and lay out all of your wishes and desires. You can work out the timing of how and when you reveal your interests as the situations present themselves. I am saying, however, that by understanding your interests as well as the interests of your wife, you will have a better chance at reaching an agreement that satisfies both of your needs.

Let's start with you. You are human. You may have said some things that you feel you must now defend. You may have entrenched yourself in a foxhole that you feel is too deep to climb out of. Take a step back and think about what you are really trying to accomplish. Look at the big picture and ask yourself, "Why did I say that? Is that what I truly need?"

Understanding your own interests will help you analyze any proposed agreement on its merits and help determine if your needs have been met. Focusing on your interests will allow you to disengage from positions that you have taken and shift gears toward what is important. You are only human and there is an element of pride involved in the negotiation. However, now is the time to look beyond your pride and focus on the ultimate goal of reaching a settlement that you can live with.

Looking beyond your own interests, let's think about your wife. Should you care about her interests? Absolutely!

Your wife might say many things during the negotiation that upset you or scare you. It will be your job to read through her words. Think about what she is really interested in. If your wife is talented at expressing her interests, your job will be easy. If your wife speaks in secret code like the majority of women out there whom we never understand, try to imagine what she is really thinking about and what concerns she has. By understanding her needs, you may be able to offer solutions that address them while looking beyond any concrete positions that she has taken.

Let me be blunt here. If your wife says that she hates you and wishes that you were dead, she may very well hate you and wish that you were dead. But during the course of a typical divorce negotiation, both the husband and the wife will take positions that do not really express their interests well. By speaking with divorcees, a number of specific issues have led to impasses which could have been viewed in terms of interests as opposed to positions. I hope that by reviewing the analysis of these issues on the following pages, you will get a better sense of how a negotiation focused on interests can help you reach your goal of a settlement that you can live with.

For each issue you will find the following sections:

1. *Your Wife Says:* Positions that a wife may take during the negotiation.

2. *She May Really Think:* True interests that potentially underlie her positions.

3. *You Say:* Positions that a husband may take during the negotiation.

4. *You May Really Think:* True Interests that may underlie your own positions.

5. *Possible Solutions:* A number of compromises that could satisfy the interests of both parties, but not necessarily their positions.

The analysis can be applied to any issue or situation.

Custody

Your Wife Says: I want sole custody of my son. There is no question about it! I am the mother. Only I can take care of him and give him what he needs.	***You Say:*** Why should you get custody? He's my son too! There is no reason that *I* should not get custody, or at minimum, joint custody.

She May Really Think: I want my child to grow up with a sense of permanence and not go back and forth every few days between homes. If the father really wants to be a part of the child's life, he will have to prove it. I do not want my child to get hurt every time the father fails to show up for a scheduled visitation. Joint custody is too confusing. What if there is an emergency? How can I make a decision quickly when I have to check everything with the father all the time? I recognize that the child is better off with two parents, but the father is just not as capable as I am of taking care of the child when he is sick.

You May Really Think: I love my son and I want to spend time with him. I know that it would not be good for the boy to have two permanent homes, but he should spend some time in my home and know my family. I don't want to be shut out of his life. I want to be a great father to my son. I might not know everything about taking care of him, but my parents could certainly help. They raised six children. I want a say in the major decisions that affect my son, and I feel that it's only right that the mother and I should be equal parents in the eyes of the law.

Possible Solutions: If we were to look only at the positions, there would be no solution. By looking at the interests, we can get a sense of what the father and mother are concerned about. In this case, both parents agree that split custody would not be appropriate and that primary physical custody could reside with the mother. The father, however, would require joint legal custody and a reasonable visitation schedule. The concerns of the mother could be addressed by including in the agreement those decisions that will be made jointly by the father and mother. Emergency decisions would be made by the parent that is caring for the child at the time the emergency occurs. The agreement could also address the plan of action that both parents would take should the child become sick when a visitation is scheduled.

Division of Husband's Law Degree

Your Wife Says: I want half of my husband's law degree. My accountant estimates its present value at $10,000,000.	*You Say:* The wife has nothing to do with my license. I earned it only a short time after we were married. Sure it has value, but she is entitled to none of it!

She May Really Think: I could care less about his license, but how will I ever get back on my feet again. I have to go back to college and earn a degree. I took care of the house while he went off to work and gain experience as an attorney. How will I manage? How will I be able to go to school and support myself?

You May Really Think: Even though I earned a law degree, I was not saving much money while I was married and I could not possibly pay a lump sum payment to my wife right now. Should I go into debt based upon my future earnings capacity? What if something were to happen to me? What if I lose my job?

Possible Solutions: It is clear that both the husband and the wife have valid concerns. The wife needs to become financially stable and go back to school. The husband is in no position to make a lump sum payment right now and is concerned about going into debt.

Assuming that the law would dictate that a part of the license would indeed be apportioned to the wife, an arrangement could be worked out where such a cost could be *spread* over a number of years. Spreading this payment would allow the wife to sustain herself and not put the husband into debt.

The amount could be based on a simple division of the wife's portion of the license by the number of months that the payments would be made. If the husband and wife are more daring, the payments could be based on the income that the husband generates from his law degree for a number of years.

The payments could also be structured as alimony, which would mean that the payments would be tax-deductible to the husband and taxable to the wife. The husband would be able to save on his taxes in the next few years while the wife may not care at all about the taxability since she will not earn enough money in the upcoming years to pay taxes.

Summer Visitation

Your Wife Says: There is no way that the child will spend the summer with you. You have enough visitation.	*You Say:* If the wife spends the school year with the child, I should spend the summer with the child. I deserve at least that much!

She May Really Think: The child is so small right now; I could not bear being away from him for a whole month or an entire summer. Maybe when he is older we could talk about it, but now is too premature. I want to make sure that he is happy and goes to a camp that he wants to go to, and is not forced to spend the summer with his father on some wild adventure.

You May Really Think: I don't see the child enough during the year, and the summer is an opportunity to do things together. I know that he is small right now, and maybe spending the entire summer with him alone would be difficult. Still, when he gets older, he could certainly spend the summer with me. He could go to camp and stay at my home. I could take my own vacation from work in the summer and we could do things together.

Possible Solutions: The positions are contradictory. The interests are very much the same. Some type of "phase in" approach could be adopted where the child spends more time with the father as he gets older. The father might spend two weeks with the son until the age of six, while the mother gets visitation one time during each of those weeks. The weeks could increase up to the age of ten, where from then on the son would spend half the summer with the mother and half the summer with the father. The interests of each party reveal the concern over the age of the son. As the father, you are right to think ahead. Your wife may be too focused on the present, but the divorce agreement should address the summer visitation for the son at all ages. The solution in this scenario is clearly grounded on a graduated schedule of increased visitation as the son grows older.

Life Insurance Policy

Your Wife Says: The husband must have a life insurance policy with the child as a beneficiary.	*You Say:* Why should I be forced to have a life insurance policy? If I want to have one, that's my business. My wife has no say in the matter.

She May Really Think: He pays child support for the benefit of our son. If he were to die, where does that leave me? I would lack the means of supporting my child and I don't know what I would do? Even if we are divorced, he is still the father and he should care about the welfare of his son, even after his own death.

You May Really Think: I have no problem having my son as the beneficiary of a life insurance policy. But I know that the money will not go to my son. He is too young to be responsible for so much money. His mother will certainly get control of the cash and do with it whatever she chooses. I should lie in the ground while my ex-wife lives it up?

Possible Solutions: It may be within the power of the law to force the father to maintain a life insurance policy for the benefit of his son. However, the amount of the policy could be linked to the actual present value of the future child support payments. Thus, as the child grows older, the required policy amount could continue to decrease until child support ends. At that point, the requirement to keep the policy would be completely phased out.

The mother and father could also agree on a trustee who would disburse the funds should you pass away. For example, it could be stipulated that a certain amount would be paid each month to the child and that specific amounts be used for education expenses or the child's marriage expenses.

Residence of the Child

Your Wife Says: I should be allowed to move wherever I want. I can't be tied down by the divorce agreement.	*You Say:* The wife cannot move away and take the child with her. The child must live close to me.

She May Really Think: I need the flexibility to be able to move if I want to. I know that my child needs a father and I don't expect to move to China or Mexico, but what if I want to buy a house in Long Island or New Jersey. I should not be locked into any one area. What if my future husband lives further away?

You May Really Think: I could not bear to live so far away from my child. I need to see her on a regular basis and spend time with her. How could I have visitation rights if she were to live so far away?
I need some type of assurance that the mother will not move to a different country or to a distant state. What if she wants to marry someone in California or Florida?

Possible Solutions: The mother is worried about being too locked in by the agreement to living in any one area. The father is more concerned with a drastic move to a far away place.
A compromise can be reached. The wife could have the right to move with the child but not to any location she might wish. Typical agreements include a mile limitation on the residence of the child, such as stating that the child could not be moved more than sixty miles from the current residence without the father's consent.

Jewish 'Get'—Religious Divorce

Your Wife Says: I want the religious divorce right now. Why should I have to wait for the civil divorce?	*You Say:* I won't give my wife the religious divorce and I certainly will not pay the amount of money specified in the Ketubah (Jewish marriage license).

She May Really Think: I want a guarantee that I will not have a problem getting the religious divorce. What if after we finalize the civil divorce, my husband refuses to give me the 'get'? I don't want to wind up like those other women who cannot remarry because their husbands refuse to give them a 'get.' I need some type of guarantee.

You May Really Think: I would love to give her the 'get.' Do you think that I want to stay married to her? I also want to move on with my life. The only problem is that I could not possibly pay the amount included in the Ketubah. I don't have any cash for that. I was very young when I signed the marriage license and I did not understand how divorces worked. Who would have thought that I would be in this situation?

Possible Solutions: This is an emotional issue for many couples. The interests of each party sometime reveal their true fears. The wife is fearful about not being given the "get." The husband is worried about having to pay the amount specified in the Ketubah. Sometimes, these two fears can offset one another and the wife might willingly forego the Ketubah money for the sake of getting the "get."

More importantly, however, is the ability to alleviate these fears by including the 'get' as part of the civil divorce, which is signed by both parties as well as a judge.

The agreement could state that the husband agrees to grant the "get" within a specified number of days from the signing of the agreement. The wife in turn could agree that all financial elements of the divorce would be handled within the confines of the civil agreement, and no additional claims will be made later on with regards to the Ketubah.

Formulating a Term Worksheet

By this point, you should have a sense of the issues that relate to your divorce. For each issue, you should understand where your true interests lie and what you would ultimately like to see in the final agreement. It is now time to organize these issues in a meaningful way by means of a "term worksheet."

When you sit down with your lawyer, he or she should ask you the following:

"What do you want to get out of the divorce? What is most important to you?"

A term worksheet will help you answer these questions and also track your issues and the progress made on each as the negotiations advance. The worksheet is essentially a list of all the topics that will play a role in your divorce. The formulation of the worksheet will necessitate that you take the following steps:

1. *Prioritize*

2. *Analyze*

Prioritize: You may find that you have ten issues to resolve or you may find that you have a hundred issues to resolve. In any event, only a handful of these issues will be of prime importance to you and should warrant the majority of your attention.

By placing a ranking next to each issue, you will stay focused on the topics that are crucial to your divorce while also identifying those issues that could be used as negotiation tools. Issues at the top of your list should be key, and you should focus your efforts on satisfying your interests for them. Issues at the bottom of the list could be put aside for the purpose of reaching an agreement.

You may decide to relax your position on item number two in order to truly satisfy your most important issue. You may decide that you will relax your position on your number one issue in order to satisfy your interests on issues two and three. Having a ranking of all the issues allows you to make these decisions and quantify what you are giving up and receiving under each agreement proposal.

The very act of ranking your issues will help you focus attention on what you really care about and help you think about what is important to you in this stage of your life. Do you care about the material possessions that have been amassed during the marriage? Are your children your priority? Is money the major issue?

When your lawyer asks you what you want, you will be able to list each issue in turn, as well as your desired outcome for each.

Analyze: Once the issues are prioritized, your next step is to analyze each one and make a number of determinations.

First, you should identify your interests. Each issue should be accompanied by a description of the interests that you have and not simply the positions that you have taken. You should not say: "I want custody" or "I refuse to pay any alimony." Instead, your interests could be, "I want to make sure that my son will have two parents and I want a guarantee that I will have the opportunity to spend an adequate amount of time with him. I want, at minimum, a joint legal custody arrangement."

You should be able to complete this section of the analysis by yourself without the aid of a legal expert, since only you can know what your true interests are and where you would like the divorce to take you. You do not have to divulge these interests to your wife or to her lawyer. These are for you. Think about what you really care about. If you want the divorce to be over as quickly as possible and are willing to pay a little extra to achieve this, that is your business. No one knows your interests except you, so take the time and figure out what they are.

Next, a best-case scenario and a worst-case scenario should be identified for each issue. The best case scenario would represent an outcome that satisfies the most interests for each issue. A worst case scenario would be an outcome that satisfies the smallest number of interests. To complete this section, you will require the help of your attorney who should be able to give you a clear set of possible outcomes for each issue and a range of expectations.

Obviously, your overall desired result would be to receive the best case scenario for each issue, but we all know that that is not realistic. The job of everyone involved will be to reach a point of compromise that they are comfortable with and can ultimately accept.

You could utilize the term worksheet at this point to track the issues that are discussed in the negotiation. You can also utilize all of the analysis that you have done so far to devise a number of possible settlements of your own that encompass all of the issues. You would try to satisfy your interests as much as possible on the issues that are most important to you, while possibly compromising some of your interests on issues that hold less weight. A compromise will be required! In order for you and your wife to agree, you will need to propose an agreement that satisfies your interests as well as hers.

A Note on *Strategy*:

How wonderful it would be if both the divorcing spouses could each create a term worksheet, sit down together and work out the best way to resolve all of the issues in an overall agreement. In the real world, this rarely would happen.

Before I get too practical, however, let me start by saying this. If you actually do have a good relationship with your soon-to-be ex-wife, as some men do, and you feel that you can discuss the issues "off the record" together, by all means you should go ahead and do so. You and your wife might be able to break through the negotiation impasses and reach agreement on the difficult issues without the help of attorneys. The lawyers will certainly advise you on the agreement that you reached, and as long as it is within reason, there would be no need for them to object. If you meet with your wife, you would be wise to ask a lot of questions with the intent of developing an understanding of the interests that she has.

Practically, however, the nature of divorce might preclude such a conversation from taking place. As such, I am not suggesting that you formulate a term worksheet and fax it in to your wife or to her lawyer. You and your attorney should make the decisions of how much of the term worksheet you will reveal and exactly when you will reveal it.

In all cases, however, the formulation of the term worksheet will help you. If you can discuss the interests of both parties in an open and honest forum, that's great, and your term worksheet will act as your guide. If you can't do this, then the term worksheet should be used as a tracking device and an analysis tool for examining proposals that are made. For each issue, you can place the actual proposal next to your desired outcome and see which issues stand out. By doing this, you can get a very good sense of how many issues have gone your way and how many have not. You can get an overall view as to whether or not your interests are satisfied and what modifications would be required to get you to the point of agreeing on a final proposal.

Creating the Worksheet

Let's walk through a simple example of a term worksheet as it evolves over time. The first step is to list the issues that you personally face.

Suppose your divorce encompasses the following topics:

| 1. Alimony |
| 2. Division of Property |
| 3. Law Degree |
| 4. Life Insurance Policy |
| 5. Outstanding Loans |

The next step is to write down your interests in relation to each issue. You can mix in some of your positions and desires, but try to focus on the underlying concerns that you have for each issue rather than just stating what you will and will not accept. In the example below I will focus my attention on the first issue—*Alimony.*

Issues	Interests
Alimony	My wife and I were married for seven years. We both worked full-time and jointly supported ourselves. While my salary was larger than hers, she too has the skills to work and support herself. While we were married, we did not live a life of luxury. Sure, we took our annual vacation, but we were frugal in our day to day lives. I would hate for the few nice pieces of jewelry that I bought her to be misconstrued as "luxurious." We were a middle-class couple, not a wealthy couple. I want to be able to make a fresh start in my life and not have to worry about making a monthly alimony payment. I hope to remarry and start a new family. If I am forced to pay alimony, I would hope that it would be minimal and for a short duration. I don't want to have an alimony payment hanging over my head for the next twenty years!
Division of Property	
Law Degree	
Life Insurance Policy	
Outstanding Loans	

As you discuss the issue with a legal expert, you should get a sense of the best-case scenario and the worst-case scenario. Realistically, the final resolution will reside somewhere is the middle of these two extremes.

Your lawyer might explain to you that although it is possible that you would not have to pay any alimony, the facts could lead a judge to allow for some payments. Your argument for not paying alimony would be based upon the fact that both you and your wife work. However, she would argue that your salary is forty percent higher than her salary, and as such, you held the majority of the financial burden during the marriage. With this in mind, a judge could decide that a reasonable amount of alimony is warranted for a number of years to even out the income and give the wife some time to get back to her current standard of living.

In any event, it would be extremely unlikely that the alimony would last for seven years, since the marriage itself was only seven years. Somewhere between one to five years would appear to be more realistic.

You can now include this information in your worksheet:

Issue	Interests	Best Case	Worst Case	Realistic
Alimony	My wife and I were married for seven years. We both worked full-time and jointly supported ourselves. While my salary was larger than her salary, she too has the skills to work and support herself. While we were married, we did not live a life of luxury …	No alimony payments at all.	Alimony payments in the amount of $1,500 per month for seven years.	Alimony payments of $1,000 per month for a period of two to four years.
Division of Property				
Law Degree				
Life Insurance Policy				
Loans				

When all of the issues have been analyzed, you can use the worksheet as a tool to either evaluate divorce agreement proposals that are put before you or propose your own package. For each issue, you can gauge whether the proposed resolution lies closer to the best-case scenario or the worst-case scenario, and whether or not the proposal is even realistic.

We will now add two more columns to the worksheet to help you finalize the analysis. One column will be titled 'Proposal.' In this column, you should write down the proposal that is currently on the table with respect to the issue.

In the last column, you can jot down any comments that you have. For example, is the proposal realistic? Does the proposal meet your interests? Also, you will want to make a note of some additional clauses that must be included in the agreement. For example, you would want to make sure that the agreement clearly specifies when and under what conditions the alimony payments would cease, and also the tax deductibility of the payments. Write down anything that you would like to discuss with your lawyer on the issue or anything that you believe should be added to the agreement.

Here is an example of a term worksheet with the issue of alimony fully completed:

Term Worksheet

Issue	Interests	Best Case	Worst Case	Realistic	Proposal	Comments
Alimony	My wife and I were married for seven years. We both worked full-time and jointly supported ourselves. While my salary was larger than her salary she too has the skills to work and support herself. While we were married, we did not live a life of luxury ...	No alimony payments at all.	Alimony payments in the amount of $1,500 per month for seven years.	Alimony payments of $1,000 per month for a period of two to four years.	Alimony payments in the amount of $1,200 for a period of two years.	Should try to get it down to one year. Also, try to get the amount down to $1,000. Prefer this to the 'realistic' case since it is only for two years. Check that the payments are tax deductible. Make sure agreement specifies when it would cease and under what conditions. Overall, should not cause an impasse.
Division of Property						
Law Degree						
Life Insurance Policy						
Outstanding Loans						

Not every issue will go your way. On the other hand, if you find that every issue is heavily skewed toward your wife, you know that you have a problem.

There is nothing wrong with shooting for the stars, but at the end of the day, both you and your wife will need to make some concessions and compromises to arrive at an agreement that you will both be able to live with. The term worksheet is a tool to help you look at each issue in detail as well as the overall agreement at a higher level. When you reach the point that you believe the agreement meets most of your interests, is realistic, and consistent with what the law would dictate, you should be very close to finalizing the divorce.

As the divorce proceedings progress, don't be afraid to modify or enhance the worksheet. If you find that every issue is skewed toward your wife, it could mean that the proposal is not realistic, but it could also mean that your expectations were not realistic. Perhaps you misunderstood the law on some of the issues and are incorrectly assuming that a proposal is preposterous, when in fact it is reasonable.

If, on the other hand, you find that all of the issues are going your way, this could signify a number of different root causes. It is possible that you are just lucky and that your wife has an incompetent attorney. This is unlikely. It is also possible that you and your wife had very different interests and that the agreement satisfies your interests in different ways. It would be great if that were the case. It is also possible that you missed something important in the agreement. Perhaps your worksheet does not include an issue or perhaps you have sold yourself short on the realistic outcome of a number of issues. Take a closer look and see if any modifications are called for.

CHAPTER 6

▼

GETTING THROUGH THE TOUGH TIMES

There is only so much that you can do from a practical standpoint. While you will spend a great deal of time with your lawyer and in the courtroom, you will also have plenty of time to think about the divorce and the next stage of your life. There will be some tough times ahead, possibly tougher than any you have experienced before.

This chapter focuses on how you handle yourself during this time and how you view the overall divorce. Is this the end or the beginning? Will you crumble under the pressure, or will you persevere? How will you manage to stay afloat?

How you think is everything, and in this chapter I offer some advice on ways to cope with and overcome your seemingly bleak situation.

Let me start by making the bold statement that *"You Are a Man."*

That's right, a man. Men persevere. Men find ways of getting out of tight spots. Men grow stronger with adversity. And men never give up. You too will emerge from this, and you will be able to hold your head up high again.

Everyone goes through ups and downs in life. Right now you are certainly down, but you will get up again, and how sweet your life will be when that happens. You only need to be patient, make it through this period and look forward to some new beginnings that you will embark upon in the future.

Despite all that has happened to you, you will come out of this divorce alive and well. You will be stronger, wiser and better off after the divorce. I know this because I have seen so many come out of divorce stronger than they were before. All men who survive a difficult time in their lives come out of the experience with a new perspective. You will be pushed to the limits, but you will not break.

The problem is that right now you can't see any of this or even begin to visualize it. You are so wrapped up in the proceedings that you are overwhelmed. You can't begin to imagine that any good can come out of this. How could you? You are in the middle of a living hell, one that you could not have ever imagined! But knowing in your heart that there will be an end to this madness and that you will come out of it standing on your own two feet will help you get through this time and look forward to the next stage of your life.

There is no way that you can fail because there is too much at stake. Your entire life is on the line here, and it's up to you to see to it that you live it to the fullest.

We are all unique, but every single one of us is united in the fact that we possess within us more strength than we can even imagine and the ability to make it through the difficult times. I know that you will make it through as well.

Forgive Yourself

I had a friend named Jim who used to work in my office. One day, I noticed that his mood at work had changed. He was sulking all the time and he seemed depressed. I wondered what was going on.

I asked a fellow co-worker what had happened, and I learned that Jim's wife had cheated on him and that he was now involved in a messy and emotional breakup. I felt terrible for him at that moment, but I also hated to see him in such bad shape. Jim spent his time agonizing over what had happened and complaining to his friends about his wife. He stayed that way for two years before he was finally able to pull himself out of his funk.

Jim had a choice. He could have chosen to move on with his life and stay positive. He could have spent his time thinking about the things that he would accomplish and the good times that he would have. Instead, he chose to focus on the past. He decided to spend his time thinking about all that he had lost and put all of his energy into negative feelings.

You too may feel overwhelmed by the situation. You may think that your life is over. I am telling you that you have a choice. You have the power to choose the way that you will react to the situation, and you can choose to recover quickly.

There are two clear roads from which to choose. You can either get depressed and obsess over the past or look ahead toward the future.

I suggest that you look ahead. The past can't be changed, and it will not do you any good to spend your time on what has already happened. What will you gain today by being too hard on yourself? How will remonstrating over the past help your life now?

Instead, push yourself to look toward the future, and to do this, you first need to *forgive yourself.*

Forgiving yourself means that you recognize that perhaps you could have done things differently, but that for whatever reason you simply did not. The most important thing for you to remember and keep reminding yourself of is that you are human, and like all humans you make mistakes. If you knew then what you know now, things might have been different. The knowledge that you have today is completely different from the knowledge that you had two years ago, and what you knew two years ago is not comparable to what you knew five years ago.

We learn from experience, and we learn the most in life by making mistakes. You took a risk and got married, and unfortunately things did not work out. You can walk away from the experience with a new perspective on life and a wealth of experience, or you can waste the next few years beating yourself up for the mistakes that you made. Before you can move on with your life, you need to take the first step and forgive yourself for whatever you have done.

There will be enough people who will be hard on you. There will be those that blame you for the divorce. There will be enough bad blood between you and your wife and possibly other family members to last you a lifetime. And there will be vultures who will try to take advantage during your time of weakness and vulnerability. Why should you join them and gang up on yourself? You need to stand up and support yourself! Start the process by forgiving yourself for the mistakes that you have made in the past and learning from the experience.

Now let's walk through a few possible scenarios as to how the marriage ended and discuss why in each case you are better off forgiving yourself and moving on with your life rather than remaining stuck on the past.

Suppose that you wanted the marriage to end and initiated the divorce. You and your wife might have changed so much as individuals in the years following the marriage that you felt that you were just not compatible anymore. Maybe you realized that you just did not love her and that you both would be better off apart.

While the divorce process will still be difficult, you clearly should be in a strong position to move on with your life and focus on the future more easily than men who did not instigate their divorces. Assuming again that there is no chance for a reconciliation to take place, you must step up and live with the decision that you made. You were the one who initiated the divorce, and now that it's underway, there is no point in second-guessing yourself.

The problem that you face in this situation, however, is one of basic human nature. When we think back on different times in our lives, we romanticize. We focus on the good times and forget about the bad. These bad times fade away into oblivion, and after a while you might be asking yourself, "Why did I do this?" In His ultimate wisdom, God inscribed this ability to forget into our souls so that we simple human beings could overcome painful events and continue to live despite sorrow and catastrophe. We blot out the bad and convince ourselves that what we once had was the greatest! "Paradise Lost," we bemoan.

Don't fool yourself! Think about the reasons that you initiated the divorce and the unhappiness that you felt during the marriage. If you are second guessing yourself, remember all of the times that you could not bear to be in the same room with your wife. Remember all the times that you felt that you were lost and confused. Remember the feelings of despair that you felt when you realized that you had made a mistake in marrying this woman. Learn from the experience. Accept the decision that you made and move on to bigger and better things.

Let's look at the flip side of the coin. Your wife decided that she wanted to get out of the marriage. Perhaps she met someone else and fell in love with him. Perhaps she felt that you and she were not compatible or that she did not love you the way she used to. The divorce itself will be difficult to deal with, but perhaps even more difficult will be your feelings of rejection and disappointment.

I know that this is a hard situation to accept and many men will blame themselves for what happened. But let me tell you that you are better off now than when you were married. You cannot change the marriage at this point. You cannot return to the past and make things better. And more importantly, you cannot dictate what your wife feels. Would you be happy living with a person who did not love you? Would you want a wife who did not have feelings for you? You shouldn't! You will be better off without her. You now have the chance to go out into the world and find someone whom you can truly love and who reciprocates your love. You can find a woman who will be loyal to you. Don't waste your time thinking about your now ex-wife and what she is doing to you. She is doing the greatest kindness by revealing her true feelings. I'm sure it hurts to hear, but it is better to hear it than to go on living in a world of make believe.

In hindsight, there may be things that you should have done differently. There could have been ways for you to keep the flame alive in the relationship. Take all that you have learned with you, and I guarantee that you will have opportunities to utilize this knowledge in the future. You will need to combat feelings of loneliness and rejection for a while, but know that you will be better off after the divorce and think about the good times that you will experience in your lifetime.

If you cheated on your wife, you may believe one of two things. You could accept the fact that you were so unhappy with the marriage that you needed to find something different. If this is the case, you would probably welcome the opportunity to get divorced and you may be the one to initiate the process, unless your wife caught you and threw you out. Alternatively, you may feel that you have made the biggest mistake of your entire life. In this case, you must forgive yourself. You are human. You made a mistake, and your life will change because of it. Be a man and live with the consequences of your actions. You took a risk, and now you are paying the price. I have news for you—if life were so great at home, then you probably would not have cheated on your wife in the first place. You can learn from the mistake that you made, but now is not the time to dwell on your error. Accept your fate, forgive yourself and move on.

If your wife cheated on you, the divorce will be the best and most logical thing for you to work on right now. Of course you will be hurt by the fact that you were betrayed by the woman who pledged herself to you, but what should you do about it now? Do you want to live with a woman who has given herself to another man? Should you belittle yourself and allow your wife to walk all over you? Should you blame yourself for her deceitful action?

I would hope that you would answer an emphatic "no" to all of these questions. Why should you blame yourself? She is the one that left you and now she must live with that.

If you have children, of course you can maintain a civil relationship with the mother for their sake. But you have every right to dissolve the marriage if that is the only remaining option. You should not blame yourself for what happened or spend time dwelling on a romanticized version of your marriage.

In all of these cases, you are better off forgiving yourself for the mistakes that you have made. You will gain nothing by dwelling on the past and berating yourself for being human. For now, you have a job to do and you need to focus your attention on finalizing the divorce and reaching an agreement that satisfies your interests. You can't afford to waste any of your energy on negative thoughts or feelings of despair. Begin the process of recovery today by forgiving yourself for the mistakes that you have made.

Focus on Survival

We all need to feel a sense of accomplishment once in a while. We men especially need to feel that we are doing something with our lives and moving forward toward a goal.

How difficult it is then for men to deal with the divorce proceedings! Think about all the time and effort that you will put into the divorce. You will expend so much of your energy on finalizing the divorce. What have you accomplished? At the end of the day you will be able to say that you are no longer married. I'm not sure that this accomplishment will give you the sense of satisfaction that you were looking for.

Many men have a hard time during the divorce proceedings since they feel that their lives have come to a halt. They work toward a goal that will ultimately translate into the cessation of a marriage in which they invested years of their lives. For this reason, it is important to acknowledge that your job right now is to "survive." You want to come out of this divorce in a position that will allow you to enjoy life at some point in the future; but there certainly will be a slowdown or even stoppage of advancement. Surviving the divorce is an accomplishment in itself, and the aspiration to survive can help you through some of the tough times when you feel that your life is on hold.

I went through some of these tough times. As a man, I know how you feel. When I was getting divorced, I felt that my life was at a complete halt. I could not believe that it had come down to this. But I told myself over and over again that now was not the time for me to accomplish great things or take on any huge risks. Now was the time to survive at all costs. I knew that there would be time enough for me to do things in life that I had always wanted to do, but my focus throughout the divorce was on surviving. This was my goal, and this was my accomplishment. *And it is an accomplishment.* How many people have gone through a divorce and been unable to function during and after the process? How many men have spent years recovering from a divorce?

Surviving means that you are able to keep your head up. Surviving means that you are able to maintain your job and that you do not allow the divorce to ruin other areas of your life. Surviving means that you might not go out as much as you were accustomed to, but that you maintain good relationships with the people that you love and care about. Surviving means that you act wisely when negotiating the divorce agreement or proving your own case in a court of law. And surviving means that you come out of the divorce ready to start a new life.

Divorce is a stressful time in any man's life. You should do everything in your power to avoid adding stress from any other of life's stress inducers, such as changing your job, buying a new home, or taking out a mortgage.

If you are established in a job but feel dissatisfied, my recommendation is for you to stay put at your current position until the divorce is finalized and then look to make a move.

If you had to leave the marital residence, think about the best way to live during the proceedings without adding too much stress. If you are able to move in with a relative, such as your parents or a brother, you may want to take advantage of that opportunity. Now might not be the best time for you to buy a new house. You may be better off renting an apartment for a year or two until things smooth over and you are able to get back on your feet again.

If you are hot tempered, now would be the best time for you to cool off. You must try to maintain good relationships with those around you. You can't use the divorce as an excuse to abuse others or take out your frustrations on them. The worst thing that could happen to you is that in addition to the divorce you wind up alienating friends or co-workers. Think about what would happen if you were to lose your job now? How would you manage?

Don't let it happen to you. Don't take unnecessary risks today. Tell yourself that your number one priority is to survive this divorce and land on your own two feet. It is a major accomplishment and you should be proud of yourself. Allow your life to slow down a bit and do not get down on yourself when this happens. Let your job be monotonous. Ride out the storm and stay alive so that you can live to see a better day. On your road to survival, it will be important to develop a support network, or a select group of individuals who will be there for you in your time of need. The network could be comprised of family members or close friends who are willing to stand by you no matter what. You may ask someone to accompany you to court. You may have to ask someone to lend you some money to help you out in a desperate situation. Or you may simply need a friend to talk to and hang out with. In any event, you want to know who your friends are and who you can really count on.

But be ready for disappointment. It is easy for people to act as friends when things are going great in your life. When you are on top everyone wants to spend time with you. In your time of need, however, things might change. Not everyone wants to be around you the way they used to. Not everyone wants to be your friend and help you out as much as you thought they would.

Don't despair. Now is the perfect opportunity to find out exactly who your real friends are and who will abandon you in your time of desperation. You will find that some people that you considered to be your best friends are not friends at all. At the same time, you will be able to see clearly who your true friends are and cherish them.

The same holds true for family members. Not every relative of yours will be supportive. I thank God for those that were supportive of me and who stood by my side when I needed their help the most. I also found out that some friends and relatives were not true friends at all. They took my divorce as an opportunity to abandon me. I can't blame any members of my wife's family for deciding not to speak with me after the divorce. After all, sometimes you have to take sides. The abandonment of members of my own family hurt far worse.

There are only a few moments in life when the truth comes to the surface, and those moments can never be taken back or revisited. What you do at those times define who you are and what you want out of a relationship. I learned a lot during my divorce. I learned who I could count on. I also learned some things about friends and family members who were not interested in helping me or lending me a hand. I don't hold anything against them. I am sure that they are busy with their own lives and I would not have wanted to disturb them. Good luck to them.

Find out who you can count on and whom you cannot as early as possible in the divorce. Utilize your support network throughout the divorce and allow others to help you. You will need them now more than ever.

Spread Your Costs, but …

The financial burdens that a divorce can place on a man are overwhelming. When you add up all of the costs, it may seem that there is just no way to make the payments. This holds especially true when looking at payments imposed upon you that are one-time, lump sum costs. For example, a division of property resolution might dictate that you pay half the value of an asset to your wife, or you may be required to pay your wife a portion of the calculated present value of a professional license, with figures reaching into the tens of thousands of dollars. Legal fees as well can seem insurmountable as they continue to pile up at alarming rates.

How can you be expected to make so many payments? In your current state, how could you possibly meet these obligations and support yourself at the same time?

In most cases, you won't have to. The best way to alleviate these fears is to focus on your responsibilities on a month-by-month basis and ***spread your costs*** over a longer time frame. This may mean that you will have to make some payments for a while, but it could also mean the difference between surviving and going under in the short-run.

Of course it would be great if you were able to get your wife out of your hair and pay her what you were ordered to pay up front. If you have a tremendously large savings account or a rich uncle who wants to help you out, go ahead and pay her today.

Most of us do not have this luxury. We need to be able to support ourselves, pay off our debts and also make the required payments to the ex-wife as set forth in the divorce agreement or the judgment of the court. The only way that we can do this is by spreading the costs over longer time spans. The goal should be to spread the costs to the point that you are able to make reasonable payments to all of your creditors while also maintaining a reasonable standard of living for yourself. I am certainly not suggesting that you push off making payments just for the sake of doing so. You should always try to pay off your debts as early as possible. You should, however, be primarily concerned with surviving, and this may necessitate that you spread some costs. You will be asked by your wife or the judge to justify your position on why certain costs should be spread, and to do so will take some analysis on your part.

Start by calculating your ***net*** salary per month. Although the gross salary will be used to calculate some of your statutory payments, your net salary, which is your salary less all deductions from your paycheck like taxes and medical insurance, is more appropriate for calculating your true disposable income. Your net salary presents a clearer picture of how much money you actually have available for making your payments. Next, estimate how much you will need to survive on your own. As discussed in the section on "Getting Organized," you will have to remember all of the costs that you incur on a monthly basis. Your net monthly salary less your own reasonable monthly costs leaves you with a net income figure, or the amount that is available to you for additional payments.

When you look at the expenses that you will now assume as a result of the divorce, include all costs including child support, education, child care, alimony, and legal fees. Costs related to a child are usually expressed in monthly terms, so they can be deducted from your net income. Other costs should then be divided into monthly amounts. You can only make payments up to the point that your net income is reduced to zero. Let's look at an example.

Suppose that your net salary is $4,000 per month. You estimate that your own costs, including rent, food, clothing, etc. amount to $2,000 per month. That leaves you with $2,000 available for additional payments.

Net Salary:	$4,000
Monthly Expenses:	<u>$2,000</u>
Available:	$2,000

There are children involved, and your wife was awarded alimony for three years and a portion of your professional license in the amount of $40,000. You also have legal fees amounting to $16,800. If you have no additional savings, you should use a starting point of $2,000 and negotiate with your lawyer and your wife a method of paying off these debts through monthly payments. If your lawyer agrees to accept monthly payments of $700, you will be left with $1,300 for payments to your wife. The legal fees would then be paid off over a period of twenty-four months. The payments in lieu of your professional license could be spread over five years, amounting to monthly payments of $666.67. That leaves you with $633.33 that could be used to make alimony payments for the next three years.

Net Salary:	$4,000
Monthly Expenses:	<u>$2,000</u>
Available:	$2,000
Legal Fees:	$700.00
License:	$666.67
Alimony:	<u>$633.33</u>
Total Payments:	$2,000

Your current assets and liabilities will be taken into account and your monthly expenses will be scrutinized for reasonableness. There's not much more that your wife or a judge could do and you can't be expected to pay something that you just don't have. If you gather the supporting documents that you need, reasonableness usually prevails and a request to spread your costs should be granted. Your wife will want to get the money somehow, and if it means that she will have to wait a little longer, so be it. Your focus should be on surviving this period of your life and guaranteeing that you will not crumble under the financial pressures of the divorce. Spreading your costs and keeping your attention on a monthly budget of income and expenses will help you do that.

See an End in Sight

As you spread your costs and focus on surviving, you will also find that you can see a light at the end of the tunnel. Your costs will slowly but surely be phased out. This provides you with the psychological benefit of knowing that you have something to look forward to, despite the financial struggle that you now face in the short-term. No matter what the current situation is, it is helpful to know exactly when certain payments will cease and when you can begin to spend more and more of your hard earned money on things that are important to you and you alone.

Spreading your costs allows you to make your monthly payments while also establishing an amortization schedule for the debt. You should be able to clearly understand how much and for how long each required payment will be made. As each cost comes to an end, you can view this event as a pay raise or bonus.

Let's just take one more look at the example provided above. After two years, you will have satisfied your debt to your lawyer and you can finally stop making the monthly payments of $700. This leaves you with $700 more in your pocket every month, and this amount of money can certainly go a long way.

The next year, your alimony payments will cease and you will have an additional $633.33 in your pocket. Finally, after just two more years, you can stop making payments to your wife in lieu of your professional license, and you will get an additional monthly bonus of $666.67. Not a bad addition to your paycheck. You can celebrate the bonus and treat yourself to something special that you have been waiting to buy. You can begin to invest more into your own future or become more speculative in your current investments. The point is that you have something to look forward to, and this anticipation should help you get through some of the financial rough times. As the payments come to an end, your financial burdens should ease and you can begin to feel more of the freedom that you strive for.

The combined sections of "spread your costs, but" and "see an end in sight" highlight the delicate balance that you must reach between maintaining your own lifestyle in the short-term and establishing a point in the future when you can see an end to all of the madness and finally began to experience some financial improvement. While you may want to simply pay off your wife right now to get her out of your life, you probably will not be in a position to do so. You need to find the balance that will work for you. If you are more worried about the next two or three years, you should try to make lower payments over these years in lieu of making those payments for a longer period of time. If you are willing to sacrifice in the short-term for the benefit of terminating your payments as early as possible, increase your monthly payments and see to it that they end sooner rather than later.

If your child is very young, it is hard to imagine that child support payments and educational expenses will one day come to an end. The truth is that eventually they will, but being a dad will never come to an end. When it comes to your kid, I recommend that you not try to calculate the end of the payments or 'see an end in sight.' Children grow up so fast anyway that by the time you stop making payments you probably will wish that you were still required to. Know that your payments are going toward the child's needs and give him or her all the love in the world, but don't spend your time thinking about when you will stop making child support payments.

CHAPTER 7

▼

BEYOND SURVIVAL

As you go through the divorce process, your relationship with your soon to be ex-wife will be strained. How could it not be? You are putting an end to something that you have both invested so much time and effort into. There is so much pain and hurt floating around that it may seem at times that you are unable to hold even a simple conversation with her.

In an ideal world, both the husband and wife will understand that the divorce must be for the best and they could decide to remain friends. In reality, this rarely occurs. What should you expect the future relationship to look like? How should you behave and treat your ex-wife?

The answers to these questions are not simple, but there are some general guidelines that you should follow. While I believe that it is in your best interest to always maintain a civil relationship with your ex-wife, if not simply for your own piece of mind, there is a specific circumstance that *necessitates* that you do so. This applies when there are **children** involved. With this in mind, this section deals separately with the cases of a couple who have no children and a couple who do. The relationship between them in each case will be different.

Suppose that a husband and wife have decided to divorce, and they had no children together during the marriage. Of course it is in everyone's best interest to try to be civil to one another. You do not have to act like the best of friends. You do not have to keep in touch and share secrets. You should be polite and courteous, because the alternative will get you nowhere.

The truth is that you probably will not have to see your ex-wife too often once the divorce is finalized. If you have to make any payments, you can send her a monthly check in the mail. If you have to divide property, you should do so as quickly as possible. I recommend that you always bring someone along with you if you are going to her home so that you have a witness just in case something unexpected occurs.

After that, there should not be many opportunities for you and your ex-wife to see one another. It's best that you both move on with your lives, accept what has happened, and learn for the future. You will not gain anything by fighting with your former spouse. The best thing that you can do is keep your dignity and walk away as a man, with honor and respect for both you and her.

This holds true for your inner feelings as well and not just your actions. What will you gain by trying to hold on emotionally to your ex-wife or by harboring feelings of hate or revenge toward her? It's just not worth it! Let it go and focus on your life. Concentrate on making your life more productive and let go of the hatred, hurt, and anger. You have suffered enough. Wish her good luck and happiness in the future, and then let her go.

While it is in your best interest to separate from your ex-wife on civil terms, as long as there are no children involved, you are really free to do whatever you want. Only you two are involved, so if you want to hate each other and fight over petty things for the rest of your lives, go ahead and see if anyone cares. You will be wasting your time and energy, but it's your own life, and the choice is yours.

I *do* care about the children who are also suffering through this divorce, and I do not want them to be hurt any more than they already have been. If there are children from the marriage, you do not have the freedom to act in any way that you see fit or to treat your ex-wife in a disrespectful and degrading manner. You no longer have the ability to choose to never speak to her again. You lost that choice when your child was conceived. There is no longer a relationship between a husband and a wife at stake. The relationship that counts now is between a father, a mother and a child, and so much more is at stake than your own feelings or your ex-wife's feelings.

Think about your children for a minute. They are going through a hard time already. They may feel that the divorce was their fault or that they could have been better kids. They may feel guilty over things that they have done or depressed over the fact that their mother and father cannot find a way to live together or be the united family that they once were. Even more so, the children will feel lost and uncertain about what the future holds. Where will they live? Who will they spend time with? How much will their lives change?

At this time, your children need lots of love and support. They need to be assured that both of their parents love them and that their own actions in no way were responsible for the divorce. They need to know that no matter what will happen, they will always have two parents who love them and who will be there for them.

With this in mind, imagine the damage that you and the ex can inflict upon your children by arguing in their presence or bad-mouthing one another. The children could be traumatized if they see their father and mother spewing venom. It is clear that overt battles between the father and mother in the presence of the children can be hurtful. But that's not all. Some parents think that if they don't scream, they are doing enough. They feel that they are allowed to hate each other, ignore one another, and treat one another with disrespect. Although such actions might not be so obvious, the children will sense the tension and it will negatively impact them just the same. Remember, children are generally more perceptive than adults. They can read between the lines and understand the subtleties of the relationship between their father and mother. If you and your former wife harbor negative feelings, your children will know it and it will hurt them.

If you and your ex-wife are thinking about the needs of the children and looking after their well being, you will both have to make an effort to behave civilly, at a minimum. You both should agree to the following:

1. *Never argue in front of the children.*

2. *Never discuss legal matters in front of the children unless their input is required.*

3. *Never raise your voice at one another in front of the children.*

4. *Always act respectful toward one another in front of the children. You can even act friendly toward one another if possible. Remember that you did love each other at one point.*

5. *Think about the interests of the child first. It's not only about what you and your ex-wife each wants. Think about what the child wants.*

6. *Don't use your children as bargaining chips in the divorce.*

7. *Don't speak badly about one another. This usually backfires anyhow, and the person doing the bad-mouthing is the one who suffers.*

If you feel that you hate your ex-wife and simply cannot be in the same room with her, do everything in your power to control yourself for the sake of the children. Use the children as an inspiration for letting go of your hate and feelings of revenge.

What do you do if your ex-wife won't play by the rules? What if she initiates arguments in front of the children and refuses to treat you like a human being?

Although it will be difficult, you need to be the man and do what's right. No matter what she says or does, continue to say, "I will not discuss this in front of the children." When provoked, tell her that it is not appropriate to fight in front of the children. Remind her that only the children will be damaged by her acting in such a way. Hopefully, this will bring her back to her senses, and you will both be able to agree on some reasonable ground rules on when and how the children should be involved in disputes. If all your efforts fail, you may be forced to seek a legal remedy by bringing the matter to court, but I pray that it should never come to that.

To recap, you are always better off taking the high road and treating your former wife in a civil manner. She is a human being no matter what she has done to you and you will gain nothing by treating her poorly.

If you have no children, you can only hurt yourself by harboring negative feelings toward your ex, but you can choose to do whatever you like. If you have children, you have no such choice. Grin and bear it. Learn to create a civilized relationship with her for the sake of the children alone. They have already suffered so much. Give them what they need most right now—your love and security.

We have talked about the concept of survival. Indeed, your primary concern during the proceedings should be to make sure that you keep your head up and come out of the divorce alive. There is so much more to life than simply surviving, however. It may be hard to realize today, but there is still some happiness set aside for you in this world; to merely survive would not be doing justice to your existence. As you begin to reach the conclusion of the divorce proceedings, you should shift your focus to enjoying life again, and this section will provide you with some helpful ways to view the divorce that should set you on the right path.

It is easy to reflect upon all that you have lost by the divorce. We all feel some level of guilt and ask ourselves what we could have done differently. I myself know the pain of divorce and I will never belittle it in any way. Indeed, a divorce is a sad event in our lives and it initially represents destruction and death. We think that we have lost our entire future and we lose hope.

There is a flip side to the coin, however, and as you begin to accept the divorce and all that accompanies it, you must consider all that you have gained and the opportunities in life that you now have.

You now have the opportunity to enjoy life again. Think about all of the pain that you have endured toward the end of the marriage or during the marriage itself. People don't just wake up one day and decide to get divorced. There must have been some issues and disagreements that led you to this point. I am sure that at least part of the marriage was not a walk in the clouds. If you thought that it was, you can now be thankful that you know the truth. Think about all the trouble the actual divorce process caused. How many times did you have to sit with your lawyer? How many times did you have to go to court and fight it out? How long have you waited for it all to finally end! As the divorce draws toward a conclusion, rejoice in the fact that this period of your life is nearing its final stages and you can finally move on to better things. What an opportunity you now have to start over!

How many things would you have liked to try when you were married but simply did not have the time or the money for? How many new and exciting trips did you want to take that your wife would not allow you to take? Well guess what? She is not here anymore. You are free, and as a free man shall you live. Your money that remains after paying off all of your obligations belongs to you. Your free time is yours. You do not have to answer to anyone anymore, or at least not for a while. Enjoy this time.

Are you interested in exercising more? Do you want to go back to school and earn a degree? Do you want to make a career change? Maybe you want to skydive or learn how to be a pilot. Go ahead. Take classes. Meet people. Do what you like and what makes you happy. Immerse yourself in new hobbies. Spend time with other family members or friends that you may have neglected during the divorce. You are alive and well and you have nothing to be ashamed of. Go out there and find the good that exists in life and take your mind off of all the suffering.

While you are out there enjoying life, remember that you have a different opportunity as well. It may take you a while to accept this, but you will now have the chance to find the person who is truly right for you. Every one of us has made mistakes in life, and perhaps your first choice of a partner was a bad one. Now you have the chance to choose more carefully. Of course you can choose to wait until you are ready to begin to date again and meet new people in a romantic setting, but eventually when you believe you are ready, I want you to have the hope that there is someone out there for you who will be a better match.

You are older and wiser, and your interests might be completely different from when you first got married. You know what you want out of life and you know what you are looking for in a life partner. You can find someone who has the same interests as you and who wants to experience life in the same way that you want to. You can find someone who will love you through thick and thin and whom you will love in return. There is a reason for everything in life. Accept the divorce and trust that it was meant to be. With this perspective, you will be able to look forward to your next adventure.

While we have spoken of divorce as an end, now is the time to see that there is a new beginning as well. You are a new person. When you married your wife, you joined together and formed an entirely new entity while also losing a part of your own identity. This new entity has ceased to exist, but you are back to your whole self again. You may have forgotten who you really are and what you enjoy doing. It's time to take a close look at yourself and focus on your own needs for once.

You have the opportunity to make a fresh start in life and become more of the man that you want to be. When you were married, your life may have become routine as you plodded along doing many of the same tasks day in and day out. Now you are a new man and you can choose to do things differently. Take this occasion to redefine yourself. Take the first step; it's easier than you think.

If you want to get in better shape, you have the power to do so. Go join a gym today or look into martial arts schools in your area. If you want to take on a new project, make it happen. Buy a "how to" book and get started. If you want to grow spiritually or intellectually, find a teacher. You have the power within you to succeed. Don't let anything stand in your way.

Let me conclude by wishing you the best of luck during and after your own divorce process. Keep your cool and always do the right thing.

I pray that your divorce will end quickly and efficiently. I hope that you wind up with a fair and reasonable divorce agreement.

And most of all, I pray that you survive the divorce with every fiber of your being intact and with a sense of optimism and excitement for the future. Good luck!

978-0-595-51098-6
0-595-51098-1

www.ingramcontent.com/pod-product-compliance
Lightning Source LLC
Chambersburg PA
CBHW052243290526
45785CB00016B/1271